Bible Stories for All Without the Dogma

A Part of Cultural Literacy

Kenneth E. Walsh

For Religious Nones and Believers
who would like to better understand Bible stories
and their influence on Western culture

Summit Crossroads Press
Columbia, MD 21044

Send requests for permissions to kenwalsh3@icloud.com.

Discounted bulk orders and the discounted teacher supplement may be ordered directly by e-mailing your request to Summit Crossroads Press at sumcross@aol.com

. . . .

The 196-page teacher supplement contains reading comprehension questions, vocabulary development, essay writing, discussion questions, and assessment quizzes.

Library of Congress Control Number: 2019914715
ISBN: 978-0-9991565-6-8
Cover picture: Courtesy of pixabay.com.

Publisher's Cataloging-In-Publication Data
(Prepared by The Donohue Group, Inc.)

Names: Walsh, Kenneth E., 1947- author.
Title: Bible stories for all without the dogma : a part of cultural literacy / Kenneth E. Walsh.
Description: Columbia, MD : Summit Crossroads Press, [2020] | "For Religious Nones and Believers who would like to better understand Bible stories and their influence on Western culture." | Teacher supplement sold separately. | Includes bibliographical references.

Identifiers: ISBN 9780999156568
Subjects: LCSH: Bible--History of contemporary events. | Bible--History of Biblical events. | Bible--Influence--Western civilization. | Christianity--Effect of agriculture on. | Human evolution--Religious aspects--Christianity. | Middle East--Social life and customs--To 1500. | Middle East--Economic conditions--To 1500. | LCGFT: Bible stories.

Classification: LCC BS550.3 .W35 2020 | DDC 220.9505--dc23

In Praise of Bible Stories for All Without the Dogma

A retired teacher offers an introduction to the major stories and themes of the Old Testament geared toward non-Christians...In the author's view, even among the nonreligious, one must have basic biblical literacy to fully understand Western society. Biblical references...abound in Western literature, art, and music, from Handel's *Messiah* to the Byrds' "Turn, Turn, Turn." The Rev. Martin Luther King Jr.'s powerful speech "I've Been to the Mountaintop" takes an even more poignant turn when readers understand the story of Moses' mountaintop experience in Deuteronomy. The bulk of Walsh's work walks readers through the major stories of the Old Testament in a straightforward, non-dogmatic way while providing brief historical and literary commentary for context. He also highlights important concepts and themes that run throughout the Old Testament that could be easily overlooked by those new to the Bible.

—*Kirkus Book Reviews*

... invites readers to engage with some of the foundational texts of Judaism and Christianity. Clear, inviting narrative, with helpful background information and thoughtful processing questions, helps us enter the worlds of such well-known biblical figures as Abraham and Sarah, Isaac, Jacob, Joseph, Moses, David, Solomon, and to understand why these stories have been shared for millennia.

—*Gail Forsyth-Vail, Retired Director of Lifespan Faith Engagement, Unitarian Universalist Association*

Ken Walsh, a truly remarkable and gifted teacher, introduced his inquisitive students to the riveting and inspiring stories of the Bible and the multi-faceted world from which they emerged. Whether they were about the Seven Days of Creation, Moses' Ten Commandments, or David's heroic deeds, Ken made these fascinating tales come alive for his students and enabled them to grasp the history and culture in which they were composed. He helped them to see their impact through the ages and their relevancy in our own contemporary culture. Now he has penned his years of Biblical instruction in this richly informative text, aided by insights, notes, commentary and chapter references, aimed at helping believers and non-believers alike learn more fully about the Bible and its significant impact on our Western culture. It truly is a work worthy of engaging those who want to explore the place and influence of the Old Testament stories on the world we live in.

—*Rev. Bill Watters, SJ, Founder and Past President of an inner city, tuition-free,*

Jesuit middle school and a high school for students whose families qualify for the school lunch program

Allusions to Bible stories are ubiquitous in our American culture, and yet many of us are ignorant of the stories themselves. Walsh's dogma-free book is a welcome introduction to these time-tested stories that are relevant to persons of any faith or of none!

—*Rev. Paige Getty, Unitarian Universalist Congregation of Columbia, MD*

[this book] has been a popular course in our congregation for cultural literacy around the Christian Bible. Walsh brings stories to life through the use of history, geography, cultural studies, and ethics. Discussion questions on ethical decision-making and personal application of essential questions allow deeper consideration of the morality tales within the Bible. For people who wish to better understand the Christian Bible and the application of its stories to today's world, this is the book for you.

—*Robin Slaw, MBA, MAT, Director of Religious Education, Credentialed Unitarian Universalist Congregation of Columbia, MD.*

...presents all that it promises with unusual clarity and rich but not overwhelming context. The straightforward descriptions, thoughtful questions, and helpful panoramic views of human life in these regions and times should prove of great value to educators and facilitators, as well as anyone seeking intellectual support in their journeys of faith.

—*Tara Hart, Ph.D.; Professor and Chair of Humanities; Howard Community College, Columbia, MD*

... Old Testament stories in clear, concise retellings with helpful notes and thoughtful commentaries ... a formidable undertaking, accomplished with skill and grace.

—*Arthur Trush, Retired English Teacher, Northwest High School, Adelphi, MD*

...a laid-back retelling of the stories we learned in Sunday School but with thoughtful questions which help the reader to interpret them from an adult perspective.

—*Sally Ann Cooper, Retired Science Educator, Howard County, MD, Public Schools*

... will stimulate your spirituality and increase your cultural awareness ... maps, extensive description of geography, and explanations of how Bible people forged a living ... told in layman's language with notes provided for more eso-teric ideas. Most important are the discussion questions that follow each story and invite the reader to see the story's relevance to contemporary life. [The book] succeeds in its objective of convincing all readers that reading the Bible is a valuable experience.

—Joseph Brune, Retired English Teacher, Loyola Blakefield High School

What a great, accessible resource for parents, students, and culturally curious adults alike, a most readable introduction to Old Testament stories, which con-tinue to be a font of Western literature, culture, and values! Ken Walsh, who in his years teaching gave a gift of cultural literacy, has written a book filled with biblical excerpts, thoughtful notes, maps, and questions for reflection. Ken's Bible Stories is an indispensable reference for anyone curious about the Bible.

—*Jeff Sindler, head of school, Burgundy Farm Country Day School, Alexandria, VA, and former headmaster, St. Ignatius Loyola Academy, Baltimore, MD*

I have been waiting for this book my entire career...Ken Walsh gives all people – the young and old, the religious and non-religious – a new way to access the wisdom, philosophical questions and moral lessons of this crucial text. It is es-sential reading for those looking to understand and grapple with Western civili-zation and the cultural moment we find ourselves in today.

—*Christopher H. Wilson. Head of School, The Bement School, Deerfield, MA*

Preface

Bible Stories for All without the Dogma was written for non-Christians and non-practicing Christians who would like to better understand Bible stories and their influence on Western culture and for Christians and Jews who like to know more about the history, geography, and cultural practices of the time.

With the United States, Canada, and Europe increasingly becoming a population of "Nones" (unchurched adults who identify with no religious affiliation), there is a growing number of people who may seek to understand the Biblical influences in Western culture. The key Bible stories are presented in a concise, straightforward manner without the dogma of religious denominations. A few choice passages that are timeless and touching are included. The background, themes, and universal life issues are described simply along with the evolution of humans, the impact of farming on religion, and topics such as slavery, government, transportation, trade, and culinary and cultural practices in the ancient Near East.

It is my hope that you will develop a better understanding of the Biblical stories and their influence on Western culture and explore the lessons that transcend the world's organized religions.

Supporting data:

Religious Nones include 34 percent of the millennials (those born after 1980) according to a 2015 Pew Research Center poll published in the

Scientific American, April 1, 2018. "The Number of Americans with No Religious Affiliation Is Rising"
https://www.scientificamerican.com/article/the-number-of-americans-with-no-religious-affiliation-is-rising/

Kenneth E. Walsh

Acknowledgements

I would like to thank the following people for their role and support in this endeavor.

• My students whose presence and discussion awakened me to their wide variety of religious and non-formal religious backgrounds and their need for information and a non-dogmatic instruction.

• My principal, Teresa Scott, who unbeknownst to me until I retired, was copying my Old Testament reading assignments for a Muslim student who was not allowed to have a Bible in his home. This experience confirmed my feeling that a non-dogmatic account of Bible stories was needed not just for non-religious people but also for those from non-Jewish and Christian faiths, so they might understand this aspect of Western culture without the traditional religious pitch.

• My Religion teachers at St. Pius X Preparatory Seminary, Uniondale, NY, who taught me the message of love in the four gospels, a message I believe is the most important attribute of life regardless of one's religious persuasion.

• Rev. William J. Watters, S.J., founder and former president of the St. Ignatius Loyola Academy, who was a caring leader who wanted every family to feel welcome and comfortable at the school regardless of their religious background. In my classes and my writing, I hope I have lived up to the example he set.

• My father, Edward J. Walsh, whose sense of humor, concern for the less fortunate, and long working hours I often recall.

• My mother, Madeline M. Walsh, whose strong organizational traits, thriftiness, religious devotion, and long working hours enabled our family to literally survive and then prosper.

• My wife, Mary Ellen Walsh, who has been my faithful companion for over 50 years, my strong supporter through two careers, and tireless assistant in editing, formatting, and making helpful suggestions for this book.

Table of Contents

Chronology

BCE

Prehistory	Creation stories, Cain & Abel and Noah
1800-1700	Patriarchs in Canaan (Abraham, Isaac, Jacob)
1700-1250	Israelites in Egypt (Jacob and Joseph)
1250	Exodus (Moses)
1220-1200	Conquest of the Promised Land (Joshua)
1200-1030	Period of the Judges
1100	Ruth
1030-1010	Saul
1010-970	David
970-931	Solomon
950	Queen of Sheba's visit
931	Solomon death. Two kingdoms form as Israel and Judah.
721	Fall of Israel.
587	Fall of Judah. Exile.
331	Return to Israel.

Source: *Who's Who in the Bible*, Joan Comay, p. 16-18.

Chapter 1. Background: Who are we?

The process of human evolution began nearly 4 million years ago with the early hominids (early human ancestors: upright, two-footed mammals with grasping limbs) who were 3-4 feet tall and had brains about one-third the size of humans today. The smaller brains limited their reasoning and speaking capacity. However, their grasping hands enabled them to collect food and use simple tools. Over time their brains enlarged as did their capacity to engage in more complex activities.

Types of Humans: Hunter-Gatherers
1. Australopithecine (Pronounced: aw stray low PITH uh synz)
Who are we is an interesting question. We go back millions of years, most notably to Lucy, an ancient human ancestor whose bones were found in 1974 by Donald Johanson in the Rift Valley of Ethiopia in northeast Africa. She was named Lucy after the Beatles song, "Lucy in the Sky with Diamonds," which was popular at the time. Testing estimated that she lived over 3 million years ago. She is believed to be an ancestor to today's modern humans. Subsequently, other remains have been found slightly older but estimated to be in the same 3-4 million-year old range. Lucy's discovery was astonishing at the time. She was the most complete, ancient skeleton found, about 40 percent complete. By examining her bones, they were able to determine that she was a female about 3.5 feet tall who walked upright on two legs and had a brain about one-third the size of ours. She was classified as an Australopithecine.

2. Homo Habilis

The next group of ancient ancestors was Homo habilis (handy man). They lived about 2.5-1.5 million years ago in Africa. They used simple tools, such as stone chips to scrape animal hides and cut meat. Their brains were slightly larger, about half the size of ours. Like Australopithecines, they had long arms, hands, and legs which enabled them to get around in trees and on ground.

3. Homo Erectus

Homo erectus (upright man) was the next type of humans who lived about 2 million – 100,000 years ago initially in Africa. They were more like modern humans in that they were upright; they learned to control fire; and, they communicated using language. Their body proportions were more similar to ours. Their brains were larger; they were also taller like us today. They used a more sophisticated tool, called the hand axe – a kind of three-in-one stone tool to butcher meat, dig out root crops, and cut wood. They moved out of Africa to Asia and Europe.

Just as the development of tools was revolutionary for ancient people so was the development of language and all of its implications. Hunting large animals, such as mammoths and bison, was a dangerous undertaking. The use of language would have obviously made it much easier to coordinate an attack by a group of hunters – quicker and clearer with less potential for misunderstanding than the use of hand signals and grunts. The development of language has all sorts of social implications enabling humans to form more effective bonds while not only hunting together but also sharing food with their group and discussing their constant need to move to find food.

4. Homo Sapiens

We are descendants of a subsequent group, Homo sapiens (wise man), which originated in Africa about 200,000 years ago and began moving to other continents approximately between 60,000 years ago (Asia) and 12,000 years ago (North/South America). They developed more sophisticated tools, such as fish hooks, bows and arrows, spears, and sewing needles. They were known to have created art, music, rituals, and social networks. They also exchanged resources over large areas.

4.a. Homo Sapiens: Neanderthals

While we do not know much about the religious beliefs of the Homo sapiens, two early types of Homo sapiens, the Neanderthals and the Cro-Magnons provide some clues. Neanderthals who lived about 200,000 to 30,000 years ago were incorrectly thought to have little intelligence. Hence, the derogatory use of the word, Neanderthal, to make fun of someone's abilities.

However, their brains were the size of ours. Evidence from graves of arthritic Neanderthals indicate they cared for their sick and injured. The arthritic Neanderthals would not have lived as long if they had to care for themselves in their state of health. Someone was feeding and caring for the injured and sick who were among the oldest people found in graves uncovered.

Their graves indicate they may have also had a ritual for burying their dead. Graves have been found with wildflowers, stone tools, and food – perhaps evidence of a religious belief in the afterlife. Tools and food would be needed in another life. In addition, they lived in large groups – about 20 to 50 people – which would indicate a need for social organization.

4.b. Homo Sapiens: Cro-Magnons

Another Homo sapiens group, Cro-Magnons, lived about 40,000 to 10,000 years ago. They are known for their contributions to the arts: cave paintings and small sculptures of humans. The large cave paintings were of horses, deer, and bison. Perhaps they were drawn as part of a religious or hunting ritual, but we do not know what they meant. Clearly, they had a sense of the world around them.

Hunter-Gatherer Summary

All of these ancestors lived by hunting animals and gathering wild food. They hunted animals, such as deer, gazelles, boar, water fowl, and fish for meat (food), for skins (clothing), and for bones (tools). They searched fields for wild cereal (e.g., wheat, oats, and rice), fruit, and nuts (e.g., acorns and almonds). Appropriately, they were called "hunter-gatherers."

The development of tools greatly enhanced their lives making it easier to hunt and to make clothing by sewing hides together. Tools enhanced their diet by enabling them to hunt a wider variety of animals and improve their chances of killing them. The ability to control fire enabled them to cook their food and keep it longer. The development of language facilitated their hunts and life together.

Agricultural Revolution

It was not until the end of the last Ice Age, 10,000 years ago, that the next major change occurred, the "Agricultural Revolution." It radically altered the lives of the hunter-gatherers who roamed the Earth for millions of years. As hunter-gatherers began to domesticate wild plants and animals, they were able to settle in one place and take advantage of a more reliable food supply. Villages of small bands of hunter-gatherers took root.

Since farming involving domesticated plants and animals could produce more food than needed, some people began to specialize (e.g., as weavers, toolmakers, potters, etc.). Small farming villages later expanded into towns and subsequently cities which provided competition among specialized workers. Cities expanded to form city-states and later they combined to form the world's first empires (e.g., Mesopotamia). With the "Agricultural Revolution" the standard of living improved from the hunter-gatherer days.

Religion

No one knows when religious practices began. Could it have started with the use of language about 2.5 million years ago? We know that the brain of Homo erectus was larger than the average brain of Australopithecine and Homo habilis. The increase in the size of human brains occurred in the region where speech is located in the brain. Or could religious practices have started with the Neanderthals up to 200,000 years ago? Was their care for the sick and injured a prelude to the Golden Rule (i.e., Do to others what you would want others to do to you) that is so common among world religions today? Was their inclusion of tools and food in graves a symbol of their belief in an afterlife, another common belief among world religions? Were the art and statues of the Cro-Magnons a symbol of religious practices? We do not know.

However, we do know that, with the development of agriculture, polytheistic (the belief in many gods) practices were common in ancient societies (e.g., Mesopotamia, Egypt, India, Greece). While the standard of living improved in agricultural societies, they were filled with dangers: flooding, drought, and pestilence (swiftly spreading infectious disease among plants and animals). These were all mysterious forces beyond the knowledge and control of people at that time. They attributed the forces of nature to different gods who needed to be pleased to avoid these unpleasant consequences. Polytheism, while it may seem unusual to many today, was the common religious practice in ancient times. The subsequent development of monotheism (i.e., the belief in one God as in Judaism, Christianity and Islam) was an unusual custom at its initiation.

Questions for Consideration/Discussion

1. Who are you? To some extent you understand your roots. However, who are you? To yourself, who are you? To your family? To your community? To the larger world? Who are you? Does the above reading help you to answer this question and understand the path humans have traveled?

2. Do you blame the forces you do not understand, such as hardships, sickness, and death, to religious beliefs? How does your understanding of your religion help you?

Chapter 2. Introduction

Numerous expressions and terms used today have their origin in Bible stories. One of the objectives of this book is to provide an understanding of Biblical (i.e., Jewish and Christian) influence on Western culture. That is the culture of Europe and the Americas. While stories are an integral part of many religions, they also convey moral lessons that are often universal or meaningful to everyone. This book explores some of these stories and the universal moral lessons found in the Bible.

The Big Questions

For thousands of years people have contemplated the big questions of life:

- How did humanity start?
- What is our spirit?
- What happens after we die?

Nearly every culture has a creation story, often surrounding a flood but not always. Faith is a belief in something even though you cannot prove it. And so, in religious faith there are many principles that we accept "on faith" even though we cannot prove them. Creation stories which predate the beginning of writing (around 3,000 BCE, Before the Common Era, or also known as B.C., Before Christ) are often accepted on faith or considered for their symbolic value. We all wonder of how humanity started. Unfortunately, we do not know with scientific certainty. However, the various creation stories provide a framework or explanation for some of us.

We sometimes struggle with the various dimensions of our spirit: our conscience, our sense of morals and ethics, and our disposition to others. Some of us find answers in organized religion; others do not. All of us think about our spirit at some point in our lives. The answers are not always clear. The issues we face are difficult at times. Hence, we struggle with what is our spirit and how to proceed.

Perhaps the biggest question for all is what happens after we die. As far back as the Agricultural Revolution and the ancient Mesopotamians and Egyptians, there was evidence of their belief in a life after death. We may imply such a belief among our ancestors, the Neanderthals, from the artifacts in their graves: flowers, food, and tools that might have been deemed necessary for the next life. Clearly, we have wondered about life after death for a long time, but we do not have any scientific evidence of a life after death. For some, their religious faith provides guidance.

Bible Background

For thousands of years during the Agricultural Revolution when large-scale, organized religion began, nearly everyone was polytheistic. It offered an explanation to why bad things happened, such as floods, drought, pestilence, earthquakes, volcanoes, disease, etc. They thought the various gods of these natural phenomenon had to be pleased or humans would suffer the consequences. Out of these concerns developed priests who could tell them what they needed to do to please the gods (usually more offerings of burnt animals and crops of which the priests were paid a portion to support themselves and their families). At this time, the gods were considered a part of the universe, not above or separate from the universe. There were gods thought to be responsible for the sun, darkness, agriculture, plagues, drought, floods, rivers, seas, weather, thunder, lightning, etc.

The ancient Israelites had an emerging, new faith that was different if not outright strange in comparison. They were a small, unusual sect that believed that there was only one God, separate from the universe. Their God was a loving God, not one to be feared or pleased but one who was concerned about the poor and the downtrodden. Out of this small group of Israelites who were just one of the groups living in the ancient Near East (which loosely resembles the modern Middle East) came a rich religious and cultural tradition that has defined Western culture in many ways.

The Purpose for Studying the Bible

Even people who do not attend church study the Bible. Why? They study the Bible to better understand Western culture, to develop themselves spiritually, and to learn from the successes and failures of others. The Bible has influenced people for hundreds of years. It is reflected in our culture, language, history, politics, art, music, and literature. Many names of people and places can be traced to the Bible (e.g., Adam, Eve, Noah, Abraham, Moses, Jacob, Joseph, Samuel, David, Solomon, Memphis, Bethesda, Jericho, Bethlehem, Babylon, Joppa, et al.)

Famous Quotes with Biblical Roots

In the past leaders have paraphrased well known Biblical passages to underscore their message. Consider the following famous quotes by Martin Luther King and Abraham Lincoln and compare them to the relevant Biblical passages.

In his famous "I've Been to the Mountaintop" speech the day before his assassination, Martin Luther King, Jr. said: "We've got some difficult days ahead. But it really doesn't matter with me now, because I've been to the mountaintop. . . And I've looked over, and I've seen the Promised Land. I may not get there with you. But I want you to know tonight, that we as a people, will get to the Promised Land." Compare to Deuteronomy 32:48-52: That same day God said to Moses, "Go to the Abarim Mountains ...climb Mount Nebo and look at the land of Canaan that I am about to give the people of Israel. You will die on that mountain as your brother Aaron died on Mount Hor because both of you were unfaithful to me in the presence of the people of Israel… You will look at the land from a distance, but you will not enter the land that I am giving the people of Israel." (GNT)

Abraham Lincoln gave his "House Divided" speech in 1858 when he ran for United States Senator. "A house divided against itself cannot stand. I believe this government cannot endure, permanently, half slave and half free…." Compare to Mark 3:24-25: "If a country divides itself into groups which fight each other, that country will fall apart. If a family divides itself into groups which fight each other, that family will fall apart." (GNT)

Notes

1.   Background: An opinion piece in the Washington Post made the case for Bible literacy with this article: Even Atheists Should Read the Bible, March 30, 2018.

2.   The Bible is one of the key influences on Western culture and its language and expressions. For example,

- References to the Book of Genesis' creation story in Milton's "Paradise Lost."
- Shakespeare's use of hundreds of Biblical references in his dozens of plays.
- The painting of The Last Supper by Da Vinci.
- In music, The Messiah by Handel.
- The song "Turn, Turn, Turn' by Pete Seeger and later by the Byrds. This song is notable for being one of a few instances in popular music in which a large portion of scripture is set to music. Ecclesiastes 3:1-8.
- The expression, "salt of the earth," found in the Gospel of

Matthew 5:13 (paraphrased).

• The saying used in many weddings, "Love is patient; love is kind. It does not envy; it is not proud." Paul's First Letter to the Corinthians. 1 Corinthians 13:4 (paraphrased).

3. More copies of the Bible have been printed than any other book and in more languages than any other book. Understanding the Bible requires knowing what the authors wanted to convey, the conditions at the time, and how the authors' perspective differs from ours today. Its message is debated. It has been used to justify wars and slavery but also to help others. It has promoted hatred and love.

Consideration/Discussion

1. What is your spirit? What religion or internal compass guides it?

2. What do you believe happens after we die? Is there an afterlife?

3. What are your favorite Biblical stories? Why are they your favorites? How did they connect with you?

4. What Biblical influences do you notice in Western culture?

Chapter 3. Geography— Civilizations, Topography and Seasons

Civilizations

Geography is the study of the earth's physical features (e.g., topography, climate, mountains, plains, lakes, rivers, seas, deltas, deserts, oases, etc.) and cultural features (e.g., language, religion, cuisine, music, customs, etc.). While the opening chapters of the Bible begin in prehistoric times (i.e., before the development of writing in 3,000 BCE), most Bible stories (i.e., Abraham through the apostles and their disciples) occur in a narrow band of written history from about 1,800 BCE to 100 CE in an area east of the Mediterranean Sea, also known as Canaan or Palestine and commonly called Israel today. (CE means the Common Era. It is sometimes expressed as AD or A.D. – in the year of our Lord.) During this time, the Israelites struggled to create and maintain their nation, Israel.

The Israelites were located between two advanced civilizations, the Mesopotamians and the Egyptians. More than a thousand years before Abraham, one ruling group in Mesopotamia, the Sumerians, had already developed the world's first system of writing, called pictographs, and later developed cuneiform to facilitate trade with a system of written records. (Pictographs consisted of 3,000 unique symbols of crude drawings. It was later replaced by a simpler, 600 wedge-shaped symbols, called cuneiform.) They had also invented the wheel, the plow, the sailboat, and irrigation. They built huge temples, called ziggurats (rectangular, stepped towers with an altar on top) in the shape that later became known as step pyramids. A subsequent ruling group in Mesopotamia, the Babylonians, under King Hammurabi, developed the oldest surviving, most organized set of laws called the Code of Hammurabi in the 1700s BCE. The Code helped him rule his far-flung empire with consistency. Everyone now knew what was expected by the king. In Mesopotamia (both Sumer and Babylonia) most people were located in the rich river valley between the Euphrates and Tigris Rivers. They were for the mainly farmers and herders.

Just to the southwest of the Israelites was another advanced civilization, the Egyptians, who had already built massive pyramids (ca. 2400 BCE) and developed their own system of writing, called hieroglyphics, and a new writing material, called papyrus (a long thin reed used to make paper-like writing material). Nearly all Egyptians were located in the narrow band of fertile land (about 12 wiles wide) along the Nile River or in the much wider Nile Delta (a triangle-shaped area of land made of soil deposited by a river about 150 miles wide and 100 miles long) where the Nile River flows into the Mediterranean Sea.

Both civilizations, the Mesopotamians and the Egyptians, had powerful kings, strong armies, polytheistic religions, beliefs in the afterlife, organized governments, and well-defined art and architecture. Despite the shortage of rain, both had successful agrarian economies made possible by their massive irrigation projects.

The Israelites by comparison were one of many Semitic speaking tribes (peoples of southwest Asia) located in the area between the Mesopotamians and Egyptians. Initially, the Israelites and their neighbors practiced polytheism as did most people of that time. The story of the Israelites unfolds hundreds of years after the peak of the Mesopotamian and Egyptian civilizations. In a sense, the Israelites were the newcomers, especially when they switched to monotheism!

The early Bible stories describe the evolution of the Israelites from one family, Abraham's, to an enslaved tribe in Egypt to their freedom and exodus to Canaan under Moses's leadership, to the formation of the twelve tribes of Israel under Jacob, and to the development of a nation (kingdom) under David and Solomon. The Israelites evolved from herders to herder/farmers, from a wandering tribe to a kingdom, from slavery to a conqueror and from an isolated group to a respected ancient world power.

Israel's Topography: The Four Topographical Zones

Israel is only 70 miles wide between the Mediterranean Sea on the west and the Arabian Desert on the east. Its capital, Jerusalem, lies in the middle of the country in the Central Mountains.

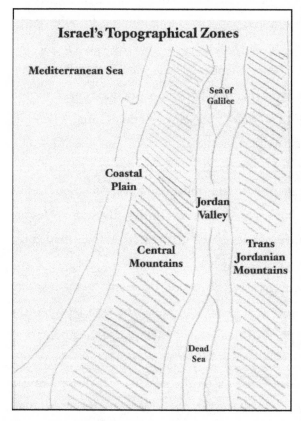

Topography from West to East
* *Coastal Plain, about 12 miles wide*
* *Central Mountains, about 36 miles wide (Jerusalem, the capital, is located here at an elevation of 2500 feet).*
* *The Jordan Valley (which is a continuation of Africa's Great Rift Valley)*
* *The Transjordanian Mountains, which rise steeply on the eastern side of the Jordan Valley and slope gradually toward the Arabian Desert*

Kenneth E. Walsh ©2019

The Seasons

Israel's people were herders and farmers. The weather influenced how successful they were. When droughts occurred, crops failed, and famine followed. For example, due to an extended drought, Jacob sent his sons to buy grain in Egypt (Genesis 42:1-3). The rainfall varies considerably in the country (i.e., more near the sea, less inland). In normal years the crops can be bountiful in fertile areas. But a multi-year drought can be devastating and cause people to move to more fertile areas, such as when Abram and Sarai moved to Egypt (Genesis 12:10). Winds bring moisture from the Mediterranean Sea to Israel. Rainfall diminishes as the wind moves inland and especially over the mountains. In normal years Israel receives 12-16" in the coastal and Central Mountain areas. (Note: by comparison the Baltimore-Washington area averages 41 inches of rain annually.) The Jordan River is used now to supply water for irrigation in the Jordan Valley. The Transjordanian Mountains are very dry and border the Arabian Desert.

Israel has two main seasons: the rainy season (winter) and the dry season (summer), separated by transitional seasons.

Dry Season – Summer (June to September)

While North Americans and Europeans experience changing weather conditions, Israel's summers are relatively stable: warm days, cool nights, cloudless skies, and rare rainfalls. Due to the lack of cloud cover, temperatures drop over 20 degrees Fahrenheit overnight. As temperatures climb in the morning, a cool sea breeze blows in and moderates what otherwise could be a scorching Middle Eastern day. On a typical summer day, temperatures begin to climb soon after sunrise. A short time later a cooling sea breeze begins to blow in from the Mediterranean Sea. The cool sea breeze reaches Jerusalem in the Central Mountains about noon and keeps the capital's temperature in the comfortable mid-80s. However, the temperatures in the Transjordanian Mountains soar into the low 100s.

What is left of the cool sea breeze only reaches there in the late afternoon by which time the breeze is too little and too late to have a cooling effect.

The dry soil in the summer facilitated travel in ancient times. Caravans and armies could move easily on the dry, dirt paths that served as roads. During the spring/summer growing season, the passing armies could also help themselves to the bountiful supply of food.

Rainy Season—Winter (December to March)

During the rainy season Israel will experience 3-4 days of rain blowing in from the Mediterranean Sea. They will be followed by a dry period. Daytime highs typically range from 50 to 60 degrees Fahrenheit and 40 degrees in the Central Mountains. Jerusalem may actually get snow once or twice a year, but it is soon gone. The winter weather can feel quite cold due to the low temperatures, the wind, and the rain.

Notes

1. The term, "Ancient Near East," covers more than the current terms Near East and Middle East. The Ancient Near East covers southeast Turkey, the east coast of the Mediterranean Sea from Syria through Canaan to Egypt and eastward to Mesopotamia and its land between the Euphrates and Tigris Rivers. The Ancient Near East was home to several ethnic groups: Semitics (based on the language spoken) including Israelites, Canaanites, Moabites, Edomites, Ammonites, Akkadians, Assyrians, Babylonians, Arabs, and Arameans and non-Semitic groups including Sumerians (part of Iraq today), Hittites (Turkey), Hurrians (NW Mesopotamia/Iraq today), and Egyptians.

2. Most of the population was concentrated in the prime agricultural land of the Nile river valley, along the east coast of the Mediterranean which received moisture from the cool sea breezes, and in the Fertile Crescent, the land between the Euphrates and Tigris Rivers.

3. Additional topographical information:

    • Coastal plain is flat and sandy with many underground springs. It was settled before the Israelites left Egypt by the Philistines in the south and the Phoenicians in the north.

    • Central Mountains are also known as the hill country. Its rolling limestone hills have an elevation of 2000-3000 feet above sea level. This is the area settled by the Israelites ca. 1200 BCE after their departure from Egypt under Moses.

    • Jordan Valley is also known as part of the Great Rift Valley which runs from the Red Sea to central Africa. It is the longest rift in the earth's surface. The Jordan River ends at the Dead Sea 1300 feet below sea level.

    • The Transjordanian Mountains, east of the Jordan River, receive little rainfall. The mountains slope gently toward the Arabian Desert to the east.

    • Southern Israel heading toward Egypt is a region with scrub vegetation fading to the desert. The region has been inhabited by nomads through the ages.

Chapter 4. Weather and Roads in Biblical Times

Roads and weather played a part in biblical stories. In ancient times, the physical features of the land influenced where roads were located. For example, near the Mediterranean Sea, roads followed the coastline where the land was flat and easy to walk. In the Transjordanian Mountains (between the Jordan River and the Arabian Desert) roads generally followed the flat mountain ridges. Weather patterns determined how people traveled and where they lived.

Weather

Rainfall or the lack of rain could pose their own problems. During the rainy, winter season roads could be too muddy to use or subject to flooding in low-lying areas. In contrast, kings preferred to go off to war during the spring-summer, dry season when roads were passable and food was available for the troops. Travel during the dry, summer season was much easier than traveling on muddy, rain-soaked roads in the winter months.

However, some water/rainfall was needed to facilitate travel in this arid, desert-like region. For example, one could not travel 600 miles straight west from Ur (in modern day Iraq) where Abraham was born to Canaan where he eventually moved because of the Arabian Desert and its lack of water and wells. Instead, travelers and traders had to follow the international trade route along the Euphrates and the Tigris Rivers 600 miles from Ur to Haran and down the Mediterranean coast 400 miles to Canaan.

Roads

The major "international highways" in ancient times were similar to the old, covered wagon trails in early American history: dirt paths following level land near water sources as much as possible and with minimal road construction. Where necessary, road building might include cutting down trees, pushing boulders/stones aside, the use of shallow fords to cross river beds, and the use of switchbacks along steep slopes. Due to flooding, erosion, and wear and tear, roads needed periodic maintenance to restore a relatively smooth and level travel surface.

Those who lived near a highway might benefit from the trade, the transportation of supplies, and the communication of news and messages. If you owned the road as some tribes, governments, and bandits did, you might earn income from tolls and from services provided, such as food, lodging, and protection in dangerous sections. However, passing armies

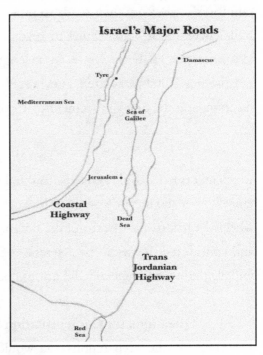

Kenneth E. Walsh ©2019

also used roads as the fastest mode of travel and attacked towns and cities and stole food along the way!

Roads also fostered cultural diffusion as different tribes and later nations came in contact and interacted.

In Abraham's time two "international highways" ran through Canaan, one along the coast (sometimes referred to as "the Way of the Sea," "Way of the Philistines," or the Coastal Highway) and the other east of the Jordan River and along the flat tops of the Transjordanian Mountains (the Transjordanian Highway).

Roman Roads

The Romans constructed longer lasting roads with better building techniques. They often leveled the road surface by flattening out hills and filling in valleys. They used flat stones as the road surface, held in place with curbing. They planned for drainage with curbs and cut-outs to move rain water away from their roads to prevent erosion and washouts. They built a network of 53,000 miles of roads which exceeded the 30,000-mile U.S. Interstate Highway System in its length. Some Roman roads are still in existence 2,000 years later! They were built to facilitate trade, communication, and the quick movement of troops to suppress revolts.

Travel

In ancient times people generally traveled by walking, including long distances. They did not ride on their donkeys. They used donkeys and solid-wheeled carts to transport goods. Because they were afraid of the sea and considered the sea to be a symbol of chaos, the Israelites were not initially sailors and generally did not use boats for a long time.

Questions for Contemplation and/or Discussion

1. Think of the preparations you would have to make to travel long distances (e.g., over 100 miles from Canaan to Egypt) in ancient times. In addition to what you may take, think about how you would travel and when.

2. How far can you walk?!

Chapter 5. Bible Organization

Organization

Although the Bible is a bound book with one cover and one title, it is not a single, unified book.

The Bible is actually a collection of many books. In fact, the word bible comes from the Greek words, *ta biblia*, which means the books. So, the Bible is like a library. In this case a collection of 66 books written by more than 40 authors (e.g., kings, poets, farmers, teachers, musicians, and fishermen) in several styles including stories, histories, instructions, letters, proverbs, prophecies, songs, and poems. They range in length from one page (2 John) to one hundred pages (Psalms). The Bible is a book about people and God.

Main Parts of the Bible

The Bible is divided into two parts: The Old Testament and the New Testament. The word, testament, means covenant or a solemn agreement between two parties. In the case of the Bible, the covenant is a solemn agreement between God and his/her people with mutual obligations. The obligations imply a strong love for each other. And to many, love is the central force in life.

The Old Testament

The Old Testament is the story of the Israelites (also called the Jews or the Hebrew people) during the time before Jesus and their unique faith in one God. For example, the Book of Genesis describes the creation of the world and the early Israelite leaders, Abraham, Isaac, Jacob, and Joseph. The Book of Exodus explains how Moses led the Israelites out of slavery in Egypt and received the Ten Commandments. Later books describe their settlement in the Promised Land, the kingdom of Israel, their exile, and their return to Israel.

The Old Testament was known as the Holy Scripture or Tanak to the Jewish people. Much of the Old Testament/Tanak looked forward to the coming of the Messiah (the hoped-for person who would free the Israelites who had been conquered by other nations).

Major Periods of the Old Testament

- Prehistory: Creation through the Tower of Babel
- Early Israelite Leaders (Abraham, Isaac, Jacob, and Joseph)
- Egypt, Exodus, and the Promised Land (Moses)
- The Kingdoms of Israel (Samuel, Saul, David, and Solomon)
- Exile
- Return to Israel

The Old Testament has 39 books which were mostly written in Hebrew. However, parts of three books (i.e., Daniel, Ezra, and Jeremiah) were written in Aramaic, a Middle Eastern language related to Hebrew but somewhat different. Jesus, who grew up in the area around Nazareth in what is now the modern-day country of Israel, spoke Aramaic.

Events in the Old Testament go back to the beginning of time which is unknown. The Old Testament ends with the Maccabean War (140 BCE). Its 39 books were written over a 900-year period between

Old Testament Timeline

	Time Period	Dates Written
First Book Genesis	Prehistory & 1800 BCE	1000 BCE
Last Book Malachi	140 BCE/CE	100 BCE

1000 BCE and 100 BCE. Writing was developed about 3100 BCE by the Sumerians to keep track of trade. About 1500 BCE the nearby Phoenicians developed the predecessor alphabet we use today.

Some of the books were written hundreds of years after the events they describe. The Old Testament stories were passed down by oral tradition until they were finally recorded in writing as late as 800 years later. By comparison the New Testament was recorded within 50 years after the events described.

The New Testament

The New Testament tells the story of Jesus, the early Christians, their new faith in one God, and salvation through Jesus. In other words, it is about a new covenant.

The New Testament has 27 books which were written in Greek at a time when Rome ruled the Mediterranean area. While many languages were spoken in the Roman Empire, Greek was a common language known to many. Greek was also the respected literary language. The most famous books are the four Gospels which describe Jesus' life and resurrection. Some of the books are actually letters, called epistles, written by early church leaders, such as Paul.

Printing

The Bible is not the oldest book even though the first book of the Bible was written 3,000 years ago. However, the Bible is the all-time bestseller with more than 30 million copies printed annually. It was the first book ever printed when it was published on the Gutenberg press in Germany in 1450 CE.

Prior to the printing press, copies of the Bible were written by hand usually by monks in monasteries. It took about ten months to make one copy of the Bible. Before the use of paper, parts of the Bible were written on stone, clay tablets, papyrus, sheepskin parchment, and scrolls.

Scrolls were stored in clay jars to help preserve them by keeping moisture and sunlight away.

Canon

Interestingly, the Bible did not always exist as the Bible. It is after all a collection of books. Both Judaism and Christianity had to make choices about which books to include and which books to exclude from their Bible/Tanak. The technical term for designating which books belong in the Bible is "canon" which means church law. Judaism did not make an official decision about which books belonged in its *Tanak* until the end of the first century CE. The Catholic Church decided which books belonged in its Bible in the fourth century CE. However, the choice of books to include was well-established by custom before the official decisions.

Hebrew canon recognized 39 books as its Tanak and divided it into three major categories:

> 1. Torah or the Law includes the first five books of the Tanak: Genesis, Exodus, Leviticus, Numbers, and Deuteronomy. The Torah is also known as the Pentateuch or the first five books. Pentateuch means five-part writing.
>
> 2. The Prophets (e.g., Joshua, Judges, Samuel, Kings)
>
> 3. The Writings (e.g., Psalms, Proverbs, Ecclesiastes)

The Christian Old Testament

The Catholic canon recognized 46 books for its Old Testament. They recognized the same 39 books that the Hebrews recognized in their *Tanak* plus seven additional books written in Greek and called the Apocrypha. The Catholics divided in the 1500s CE during the Reformation period over protests about the Pope and other issues of faith. The protesters became known as the Protestants. They selected the *Tanak* for their Old Testament. They thought it would be more authentic than the longer Catholic Old Testament because the *Tanak* was older. The Protestants hoped that the use of the older, Hebrew Tanak would give them more credibility than the newer Catholic version of the Old Testament. Today some Protestant editions of the Bible include the apocryphal books.

Time Periods in the Ancient Near East

100,000 - 12,000 BCE: Paleolithic (Old Stone Age – hunter-gatherers)

7,500 - 4,000 BCE: Neolithic (New Stone Age – farmers)

3,000 - 1,200 BCE: Bronze Age (bronze tools & weapons)

Beginning of the River Civilizations in Mesopotamia,

Egypt, the Indus Valley & China

1,200 - 600 BCE: Iron Age (stronger iron tools & weapons)

300 - 30 BCE: Hellenistic (Greek Civilization

30 - 400 CE: Roman Civilization

Finding Your Way around the Bible

Name of Book

↓

Genesis 1: 1-3

↑ ↑

Chapter: Verse(s)

Consideration/Discussion

1. Imagine yourself in the 1st century CE when the books of the Tanak were being decided or in the 4th century CE when the books of the Catholic Bible were being decided. Most people could not read. There were few actual copies of the books available. Stories based on the books and oral tradition were common. Which stories, which books, would you include in the Holy Scripture? Which would you leave not? Why?

2. Think now of all the different backgrounds of the writers and the different forms of writing. Think how their backgrounds may have influenced them.

Chapter 6. Introduction to the Book of Genesis

Overview

The Book of Genesis, the first book of the Bible/Tanak, describes the creation of the world and humans, the early days of the human race, and the patriarchs of the Israelites. The word, genesis, means origin or beginning.

The Book of Genesis is divided into two parts:

• **Chapters 1-11:** Creation stories and the stories of the early humans (i.e., Adam and Eve, Cain and Abel, Noah and the flood, and the Tower of Babel). These stories occurred in the prehistoric period. They were passed down first through hundreds of years of oral tradition. Beginning in 1,000 BCE they were written down.

• **Chapters 12-50:** The stories of the patriarchs (i.e., Abraham, Isaac, and Jacob) and Joseph. These stories began about 1800 BCE and were recorded in writing about 800 years later. However, some of these events are confirmed by other tribes' earlier writing, artifacts, and oral tradition.

Background

One characteristic of religion that distinguishes it from other studies, such as science, engineering, and history, is faith. While many elements of religion can be proven, some cannot and are accepted as faith, something you believe even though you cannot prove it.

Babylonian and Israelite Religious Views

Almost everyone, including the Israelites at one time, believed in polytheism. Ancient people did not know the science which could explain natural phenomena, such as flooding, drought, and pestilence. Since many ancient people gave up their hunter-gatherer ways for settled farming, they could not easily move from one affected area to another when a calamity struck. They associated natural phenomena such as the sun, rain, wind, stars, etc. with gods. In other words, their gods were part of the universe. Ancient people believed they had to please their gods almost slave-like or they might suffer if the gods became upset (e.g., and cause floods, droughts, and pestilence). They offered the gods sacrifices of crops, animals, and in some cultures, humans. These selfish gods were feared and were often thought to fight each other. Sometimes people felt that they were caught in the middle of warring gods while trying to please them. Not an easy task in their view! What a chaotic world it was for them.

Beginning with Abraham, although he and his successor patriarchs and leaders struggled with this, the Israelites developed a belief in monotheism, believing in only one god. Their God was different. Their God was not a part of the universe but separate from it. They believed their God was a loving God who cared about the people. And most surprisingly, they believed that humans were made in the image of their God.

Ancient View of the World

Babylonian View	Jewish View
Polytheism	Monotheism
Selfish gods	Loving God
The gods are part of the universe	God is separate from
(e.g., natural forces: sun, moon, rain, etc.).	the universe.
Humans exist to serve the gods.	Human beings are made in God's image.

Chapter 7. Creation Part One— Seven Days (Genesis 1:1-2:4)

Background

"Let there be light." So begins the famous Bible story of creation. (Genesis 1:3) (GNT)

Every ancient society had a creation story. Some of them, such as the neighboring Sumerians, may have been earlier than the Jewish and Christian creation story of the Bible. Interestingly, a number of creation stories share similar characteristics: creation out of chaos (a confusing, unorganized state) and flooding.

Creation stories try to answer that basic question we all ponder at some time: Where did we come from? In other words, how did humanity start? If God created the world, then who created God? We all ask these questions, but no one can answer them definitively. We often rely on the faith of our religion to help explain or make sense of it all. Faith is what we accept without proof usually because there is no proof to be had.

Theme

Several themes run through the Bible. The most prominent one in the Old Testament is the theme of covenant. That is, the theme of solemn agreements with mutual obligations between God and his/her people. In other words, God promises salvation (to be saved, for example, for everlasting life) if God's people do certain things (e.g., switch from polytheism to monotheism, follow God's rules, etc.) Other prominent themes in the Bible include love, mercy, and forgiveness. These latter themes have an essential bearing on our everyday life regardless of one's particular religion. They provide guidance to all of us regardless of our religious outlook.

The Story

Chapter 1: The Creation of the World in Seven Days (The Book of Genesis)

Our story begins in chaos. In the Israelites' Holy Scripture, the *Tanak* (the Christian's Old Testament), there is just a raging ocean in darkness. In the beginning, when God created the universe, the earth was formless and desolate. The raging ocean that covered everything was engulfed in total darkness. (Genesis 1:1-2) (GNT)

Day One: Light

Then God commanded, "Let there be light," and light appeared. God was pleased with what he/she saw. Then God separated light from darkness and named the light "Day" and the darkness "Night." Evening passed, and morning came – that was the first day. (Genesis 1:3-5) (GNT)

Day Two: Water & Sky

Then God commanded, "Let there be a dome to divide the water and to keep it in two separate places" – and it was done. So, God made a dome, and it separated the water under it from the water above it. God named the dome "Sky." Evening passed, and morning came – that was the second day. (Genesis 1:6-8) (GNT)

Day Three: Dry Land & Plants

Then God commanded, "Let the water below the sky come together in one place, so that the land will appear" —and it was done. God named the land "Earth," and the water which had come together God named "Sea." And God was pleased. Then God commanded, "Let the earth produce all kinds of plants, those that bear grain and those that bear fruit"—and it was done. So, the earth produced all kinds of plants and God was pleased. Evening passed, and morning came – that was the third day. (Genesis 1:9-13) (GNT)

Day Four: Specific Light: Sun, Moon, Stars

Then God commanded, "Let lights appear in the sky to separate day from night and to show the time when days, years, and religious festivals begin; they will shine in the sky to give light to the earth"—and it was done. So, God made two larger lights, the sun to rule over the day and the moon to rule over the night. God placed the lights in the sky to shine on the earth, to rule over day and night, and to separate light from darkness. And God was pleased. Evening passed, and morning came—that was the fourth day. (Genesis 1:14-19) (GNT)

Day Five: Water Creatures & Birds

Then God commanded, "Let the water be filled with many kinds of living beings, and let the air be filled with birds." So, God created the great sea monsters, all kinds of creatures that live in the water, and all kinds of birds. And God was pleased…. Evening passed, and morning came—that was the fifth day. (Genesis 1:20-21, 23) (GNT)

Day Six: Animals and Humans

Then God commanded, "Let the earth produce all kinds of animal life: domestic and wild, large and small"—and it was done….Then God said, "And now we will make human beings; they will be like us and resemble us"….So, God created human beings, making them to be like himself/herself. God created them male and female…God looked at everything he/she had made and was pleased. Evening passed, and morning came—that was the sixth day. (Genesis 1:24, 26, 27, 31) (GNT)

Day Seven: Rest

By the seventh day God finished what he/she had been doing and stopped working. God blessed the seventh day and set it apart as a special day, because by that day God had completed creation and stopped working. And that is how the universe was created. (Genesis 2:2-4) (GNT)

Commentary

Creationists are those who believe the Book of Genesis is factually correct and that the world was literally created in seven days as described in the Bible. On the other hand, evolutionists believe the earth evolved over billions of years. Some religions, such as the Catholics and some Protestant denominations, affirm the scientific evidence supporting evolution but also cherish the beauty of the Genesis account of creation. It offers a framework for understanding the magnificence of creation and the goodness of their loving God as opposed to the fearsome, polytheistic gods of the Israelites' neighbors. On a detail level, it may help to think of each day in the Genesis account of creation as a period of time and not a 24-hour day.

Chapter 8. Creation Part Two: Adam & Eve (Genesis 2:7-3:24)

Background

There is a second creation story, the one about Adam and Eve. Perhaps the two stories were written by different people and brought together by the writer compiling the Book of Genesis. Or is the Adam and Eve story simply a continuation of the seven days story with details about the first humans? We do not know! Both stories have been with us for thousands of years. They are an important part of Jewish and Christian traditions and are fondly recalled by millions.

The Adam & Eve Creation Story

God took some soil from the ground and formed a man out of it; God breathed life-giving breath into his nostrils, and the man began to live.... Then God placed the man in the Garden of Eden to cultivate it and guard it. (Eden has often been thought to mean delight or garden of God.) God told him, "You may eat the fruit of any tree in the garden, except the tree that gives knowledge of what is good and what is bad. You must not eat the fruit of that tree; if you do, you will die the same day."... God took some soil from the ground and formed all the animals and all the birds. Then God brought them to the man to see what he would name them; and that is how they all got their names...God made the man fall into a deep sleep, and while he was sleeping, God took out one of the man's ribs and closed up the flesh. God formed a woman out of the rib and brought her to him...The man and the woman were both naked, but they were not embarrassed. (Genesis 2:7, 15-17, 19, 21-22, 25) (GNT)

Adam & Eve's Disobedience

Now the snake was the most cunning animal that God had made. The snake asked the woman, "Did God really tell you not to eat fruit from any tree in the garden?" "We may eat the fruit of any tree in the garden," the woman answered, "except the tree in the middle of it. God told us not to eat the fruit of that tree or even touch it; if we do, we will die." The snake replied, "That's not true; you will not die. God said that because God knows that when you eat it, you will be like God and know what is good and what is bad."

The woman saw how beautiful the tree was and how good its fruit would be to eat, and she thought how wonderful it would be to become wise. So, she took some of the fruit and ate it. Then she gave some to her husband, and he also ate it. As soon as they had eaten it, they were given understanding and realized that they were naked; so, they sewed fig leaves together and covered themselves.

That evening they heard God walking in the garden, and they hid from him among the trees. But God called out to the man, "Where are you?" He answered, "I heard you in the garden; I was afraid and hid from you, because I was naked." "Who told you that you were naked?" God asked. "Did you eat the fruit that I told you not to eat?" The man answered, "The woman you put here with me gave me the fruit, and I ate it." God asked the woman, "Why did you do this?" She replied, "The snake tricked me into eating it." (Genesis 3:1-13) (GNT)

God Pronounces Judgment

Then God said to the snake, "You will be punished for this; you alone of all the animals must bear this curse: From now on you will crawl on your belly, and you will have to eat dust as long as you live." God said to the woman, "I will increase your trouble in pregnancy and your pain in giving birth." And God said to the man, "You listened to your wife and ate the fruit which I told you not to eat. Because of what you have done, the ground will be under a curse. You will have to work hard all your life to make it produce enough food for you." So, God sent them out of the Garden of Eden and made them cultivate the soil from which they had been formed. (Genesis 3:14, 16-19, 23) (GNT)

Notes

1. Where was the Garden of Eden?

> a. According to Genesis 2:8-14, God planted a garden in Eden, in the East, where beautiful trees and good fruit grew. A stream that flowed through Eden divided into four rivers: Ganges (India), the Nile (Egypt), the Tigris (Iraq), and the Euphrates (Iraq). (Gen 2:8,10) (GNT)

> b. Some have thought the Garden of Eden may have been located near the headwaters of the Tigris and Euphrates just southwest of Mt. Ararat in Turkey, where it has been speculated that Noah's ark landed. Another location may have been the mouth of the Euphrates and Tigris Rivers near the Persian Gulf.

2. The belief that Adam was created out of clay is similar to ancient Egyptian and Mesopotamian folk stories about creation.

Commentary

1. The story of the tree that gives knowledge of good and bad is the first of many Bible stories about testing.

2. Did God lie? God said, "You may eat the fruit of any tree in the garden, except the tree that gives knowledge of what is good and what is bad. You must not eat the fruit of that tree; if you do, you will die the

same day." Yet Adam and Eve did not die. Instead they were exiled from the Garden of Eden and had to live much more difficult lives.

Some people look at the meaning of the message here and interpret it as follows. Adam and Eve were living a perfect life with no concerns about food, clothing, and shelter. When they ate the forbidden fruit, they lost that perfect life, an everlasting life. They now had a mortal life filled with hardship and an eventual physical death. In one respect, they did die. They lost their eternal life.

Questions for Consideration/Discussion:
(Questions from Living the Promise, p. 17.)

1. Why would God put the tree there if he didn't want them to partake? Perhaps God was testing them. The concept of testing is common in many religions. Both religious and non-religious people will sometimes encounter tests of character.

2. Was the penalty fair? In polytheism the gods often use death as a penalty! This God just banished them.

3. Is curiosity a good or bad trait?

4. Are there times you should not go along with others, a leader, or an older person?

Chapter 9. Cain & Abel (Genesis 4)

Introduction

There's a lot going on in the famous Cain and Abel story. This is the first time in the Bible that we have a story about sons. In ancient cultures the older son was typically favored. For example, according to ancient Israelite customs, the oldest son would inherit a double share when the parents passed on. (If there were three sons, the oldest would receive a one-half share, and the other two sons would receive a one-quarter share each.) (Deuteronomy 21:17)

Notice who is favored in this story. Also notice that this is the first time a farmer and a herder are mentioned. Traditionally and up to modern times, these two have often been at bitter odds with each other. As you read, think of the possible options for a better resolution to disappointment. And lastly, watch how owning up and taking responsibility are handled.

The Cain and Abel Story

Adam and Eve had two sons: Cain, the older one, and Abel, the younger one. Cain was a farmer and Abel a shepherd. After some time, Cain brought some of his harvest and gave it as an offering to God. Then Abel brought the first lamb born of one of his sheep, killed it, and gave the best parts of it as an offering. God was pleased with Abel and his offering but rejected Cain's offering. Cain became furious and scowled in anger. God said to Cain, "Why are you angry? Why that scowl on your face? If you had done the right thing, you would be smiling; but because you have done evil, sin is crouching at your door. It wants to rule you, but you must overcome it."

Then Cain said to his brother Abel, "Let's go out in the fields." When they were out in the fields, Cain turned on his brother and killed him.

God asked Cain, "Where is your brother Abel?" Cain answered, "I don't know. Am I supposed to take care of my brother?"

Then God said, "Why have you done this terrible thing? Your brother's blood is crying out to me from the ground, like a voice calling for revenge. You are placed under a curse and can no longer farm the soil. It has soaked up your brother's blood as if it had opened its mouth to receive it when you killed him. If you try to grow crops, the soil will not produce anything; you will be a homeless wanderer on the earth."

And Cain said to God, "This punishment is too hard for me to bear. You are driving me off the land and away from your presence. I will be a homeless wanderer on the earth, and anyone who finds me will kill me." But God answered, "No. If anyone kills you, seven lives will be taken in revenge." So, God put a mark on Cain to warn anyone who met him not to kill him. And Cain went away from God's presence and lived in a land called "Wandering" which is east of Eden.

Adam and his wife had another son. She said, "God has given me a son to replace Abel, whom Cain killed." She named him Seth. (Genesis 4: 3-16, 25) (GNT)

Notes

1. Genesis 4:17 does not tell us where Cain finds a wife. Was she one of Adam and Eve's daughters as later Jewish and Christian traditions assume? Or was she from one of the other families created by God after Adam and Eve?

2. Genesis 4:17-22. After God punishes Cain, we learn that Cain married and that several elements of civilization develop from Cain's descendants. They include building cities, making musical instruments and bronze and iron tools.

Commentary

1. This story marks the beginning of an upcoming pattern: God favoring the younger son, in this case, Abel, over the older son. In many ancient cultures, the oldest son was the most favored. The pattern which will be developed further in future Bible stories will establish a new principle on the importance of others, not just the oldest son.

2. The ancient conflict between farmers and herders: In ancient times, there was no concept of individual ownership of property. Each person stood for a different way of life: a settled farmer or a roaming herder. Herders followed their flocks of sheep and goats or guided them to green pastures for grazing. And after a few days or weeks when the land became bare, they moved on. Meanwhile, farmers settled in one place, built a more permanent shelter than a tent, and cultivated a patch of land to produce crops. They did not use fencing in those days. However, the herder could not control each animal in his flock. Therefore, when a herder was in the area, farmers were extremely worried that their crops, their source of food for the next year, could be eaten by the herder's flock. All through history this has been a source of often bloody conflict.

3. Mercy: Cain complained that God was too hard on him. Not only will he have to work hard all his life just to find enough food to get by on, but as a homeless wanderer he may be killed by others who find him. God agreed and placed a special mark on Cain to protect him from others. We have in this story the first of many examples of mercy. Showing mercy, compassion, and kindness, these are all examples of themes repeated in

Bible stories. The ability to be merciful, compassionate, and kind are important personality traits in your personal life and on the job.

4. Overarching Point: Violence is not acceptable, no matter our feelings. No matter how hurt or rejected we feel. No matter how angry we are.

Consideration/Discussion

1. What were Cain's anger management options? How could Cain have better handled this situation?

Possible answers:

> a. Offer God his best crops. We do not know if Cain did although we do know Abel offered God the best parts of the first-born lamb.
>
> b. Trade some of his crops with Abel for a lamb to offer to God since we know that God accepted a lamb.
>
> c. Ask God what is the matter? This is perhaps the option we can learn the most from: It is best to always ask why something is not acceptable before reacting. You can always act. However, by first asking what is wrong; you are providing an opportunity for an explanation and perhaps an apology; and, you are showing concern and respect to the other person.

2. Responsibility for Special Relations/Keeping the Bond: Can you imagine giving your best friend a birthday gift and he/she just gives it back to you, rejecting your kindness? Cain may have felt the same hurt. What do you do in this situation?

Possible answer: Ask your best friend what is the matter. Although you are insulted and perhaps publicly humiliated, if you are truly a friend, you are there for him/her when he/she does something out of the ordinary. You can always react but, before you act in kind, you may want to give him/her the option of explaining and possibly apologizing. Maybe something just happened in his/her family such as a death or serious illness and he/she is lashing out in a distraught manner. Maybe unbeknownst to you, someone has belittled the type of gift you gave and your friend, in a weak moment, went along with the crowd for a regrettable putdown of your gift. Perhaps your question will make him/her aware of how painful his/her rejection was to you, and he/she will offer you a heartfelt apology. But being there for others, especially in a close relationship like best friends or spouses, is a key responsibility that is hard to do but often deeply appreciated.

3. How do you handle your anger and rejection? Life is full of small, but sometimes deeply felt, disappointments. Many of us have thought about this and developed techniques we use when we are upset. What are your anger management techniques?

4. Am I my brother's keeper? What is my responsibility?
Responsibility for Others: When God asks Cain where Abel is, Cain actually talks back to God with this quote: "I don't know. Am I supposed to take care of my brother?" (Gen. 4:0)(GNT) Did Cain take responsibility for his brother, Abel? Does he own up to what he did?
Question: Am I supposed to take care of my brother? Examples: family member, friend, neighbor, classmate, co-worker? If so, to what extent? Most of us agree that we have some responsibility for others. In fact, we have organized city, county, state, and Federal government agencies to help others in need. Some of us support non-government agencies, such as churches, synagogues, temples, mosques, and community organizations that help others. And then many of us directly help others in need, such as our family, our friends, our community, and others.

Chapter 10. Noah and the Flood (Genesis 6-9)

Background

In many ancient cultures tales of massive flooding were common. They were found in the stories of Sumerian, Babylonian, Greek, Roman, Celtic, Cameroon, Hindu, Chinese, Maori, Tlingit, Hopi, Inca, and other cultures. Since ancient people knew little about the science of natural forces threatening their survival, it was not unusual for them to attribute such forces to the will of the gods. The Noah story is one of the most famous flood stories and is full of rich symbolism that is represented in our culture today. Could the story of Noah and the Flood have been influenced by earlier myths of other cultures, especially the similar stories of the nearby Sumerians and Babylonians? We do not know.

Introduction: Human Wickedness and Noah

When God saw how wicked nearly everyone on earth had become and how evil their thoughts were all the time, God was sorry that he/she ever made them and put them on earth. God was so filled with regret that God said, "I will wipe out these people I have created, and also the animals and birds, because I am sorry I made them." But God was pleased with Noah who had three sons. Noah had no faults and was the only good man of his time. God said to Noah, "I have decided to put an end to all the people. I will destroy them completely because the world is full of their violent deeds. Build a boat for yourself out of good timber 450 feet long, 75 feet wide, and 45 feet high. I am going to send a flood to destroy every living being. But I will make a covenant with you. Go into the boat with your wife, your sons, and their wives. Take into the boat with you a male and a female of every kind of animal and bird. Take along food for you and them." Noah did everything God commanded. (Genesis 6:5-9, 13-15, 17-22) (GNT)

The Flood

Noah built an ark as instructed by God. He gathered pairs of each kind of animal along with supplies of food. When the rain started Noah, his wife, his three sons, and their wives all boarded the ark. The rain continued for forty days and forty nights, flooding the land and covering the mountains. All the living beings on earth except those on the ark were destroyed by the flood because of the wickedness on earth. Eventually the rain stopped, and the water receded.

Noah released a raven which flew around but never came back. Next Noah released a dove to see if the water still covered all the land. However, it did not find a place to land and so it came back. Noah then waited seven days and released another dove. It returned the same evening with an olive twig in its beak. Noah waited another seven days and released the dove again. This time it did not come back. Noah now thought that dry ground was reappearing again. At last God told Noah to leave the boat with all the animals so they would could spread over the earth.

Sacrifice and Covenant

Upon leaving the ark, Noah offered a sacrifice, a gift of thanks, to God for saving him and his family. God was pleased and decided to never again destroy all living things because of what people do. God then made a covenant, a solemn agreement, with Noah to never again destroy all living beings with a flood. The sign of the covenant would be the rainbow.

Notes

1. Numbers

    a. The use of the numbers seven and forty recur in Bible stories. For example, the world was created in seven days (Genesis 2:2). Noah was given seven days' notice as to when the flooding would begin (Genesis 7:4)(GNT). Joseph foretold of seven years of plentiful harvest in Egypt to be followed by seven years of famine (Genesis 41:29-30). A number of Biblical scholars have noted that the number seven was also commonly referred to in Persian, Indian, Greek, and Roman cultures and that it often was used in conjunction with the concept of completeness, fullness, or just as a commonly used, round number as we would say today about a dozen.

    b. The number forty was used in the Noah story which mentioned that it rained for forty days and nights (Genesis 7:4, 12). Moses stayed on Mt. Sinai with God for forty days and nights (Genesis 34:28). The Israelites wandered in the Sinai desert for forty years due to their unfaithfulness (Numbers 14:33). Jesus fasted for forty days and forty nights in the desert (Matthew 4:2). Many Biblical scholars view the number forty as representing a period of testing or purification.

2. Floodgates

The ancient peoples did not have our understanding of science or geography. The ancient Israelites thought that water was literally all around them. They believed that land was just a pillar surrounded by water. They thought the blue sky was a dome holding back the water above them. Rain, sleet, and snow fell out of holes in the dome. —Genesis 7:11 "When Noah was six hundred years old, on the seventh day of the second month all the outlets of the vast body of water beneath the earth burst open, all the floodgates of the sky were opened, and rain fell for forty days and nights." —Genesis 8:2 (GNT) "The outlets of water beneath the earth and the flood gates of the sky were closed."

Commentary

1. Symbols

    a. Rainbow

    The rainbow is the most known symbol in the Noah story, a symbol of God's covenant to never again destroy all living beings with a flood. Rainbows have been used as symbols in a number of cultures. For many people today, the rainbow is a symbol of hope. In addition, rainbows have been a symbol of a bridge from the people of the world to the heavens of the gods (Norse culture) , a symbol of never attainable treasure (i.e., the pot of gold at the end of the rainbow—Irish folklore), a symbol of cooperation in the German Peasants War, a symbol of peace in Italy, a symbol of gay pride and the LGBTQ movement, and a political symbol of Jesse Jackson's rainbow coalition for social justice and civil rights.

    b. Dove and Olive Branch

    The dove and the olive branch are the first symbols of peace in the Bible. They symbolize the peace that returned to earth after the flood. The dove is a beautiful, white bird. The olive tree is among the first domesticated trees. It grows well in the rocky, dry soil of the Mediterranean region. Its valuable oil is used for salad dressing, skin care, frying, fuel for lamps, and religious purposes. The Great Seal of the United States depicts a bald eagle holding an olive branch and a bundle of arrows. The United Nations Seal depicts the map of the world surrounded by two olive branches.

2. Themes of the Noah and the Flood Story

    a. Faithfulness

    God's solemn promise to never again destroy all living beings despite their failings.

    b. Justice & Punishment; Good & Evil; Reward & Punishment

    God punishes the wicked people of the world but spares Noah, the one good person.

    God decides to give humans a second chance. This concept of second chances includes mercy and forgiveness in subsequent Bible stories (e.g., in the next story, the Tower of Babel). The concepts of second chances, mercy, and forgiveness are universal moral principles common to all people regardless of their religion.

3. Creation

The story of Noah can be considered another "creation story" as the world starts over again.

Consideration/Discussion

1. In the beginning of the Noah story, Genesis 6, God saw how wicked people had become but noticed that Noah had no such faults. Question: Can one sin or misdeed lead to another?

2 Noah is described as the only good man of his time. How does it feel to do the right thing as opposed to going along with everyone else on an inconsiderate or outright, wrong path? How does it feel to be different? How do you find the strength to be different? What is difficult about being different?

3 How do you feel when you break off from your friends to do what you feel is the right thing to do? Do your friends respect you anyway? Are you made fun of? How have you handled such a situation?

4. Discuss the loneliness of doing the right thing. Noah, alone, did the right thing despite feeling different from his friends. All people go through difficult times.

Chapter 11. Tower of Babel (Genesis 11)

Background

According to Biblical tradition, the descendants of Noah's three sons spread out.

- Japheth's descendants headed north toward Turkey and Greece.
- Ham's descendants went toward Arabia, Egypt, and Africa.
- Shem's descendants settled in the Euphrates Valley of modern-day Iraq.

It has often been thought that the Tower of Babel resembled a Babylonian ziggurat, a type of stepped pyramid that was a predecessor of the Egyptian pyramid. The Babylonians built ziggurats, huge structures that could be seen for miles, as palaces on earth for the visiting gods and as temples to offer sacrifices to their gods. The word, Babel, has been interpreted to mean the gateway of god in Akkadian, the language of Babylonia.

The Tower of Babel

According to the Bible story, there was initially only one language in the world. As hunter-gatherers started farming, some settled in Babylonia. They decided to make mud bricks and bake them in the sun to harden them. They built a city, called Babylon, and then a tower to "reach the sky." This was most likely a ziggurat, a four to seven step-like pyramid that was used to worship the gods in Babylonia. They wanted to draw people together in their city with its high tower stretching toward the heavens. They wanted to make a name for themselves and not be scattered all over.

However, God was not pleased with their pride. God scattered them all over the earth and mixed up their language, so they could not talk to each other in the same language.

Notes

1. Why was the Tower of Babel story written? Some Biblical scholars have speculated that it explains why there are different languages around the world.

2 The story of the Tower of Babel ends with the pre-historic period in the Bible. That is, the period before writing.

Consideration/Discussion

1. The Babylonians wanted to build a tower to reach the sky where ancient folks thought the gods resided. Do you think they might have wanted to be as powerful as a god? Or did they just want to bring themselves together since they had settled across the land? Was there a bit of showing off, wanting to be great?

2. The Tower of Babel story is a continuation of the story of people messing up, not following the rules, or just being too self-centered as seen earlier with Adam and Eve, Cain and Abel, Noah's neighbors, and now the early Babylonians. Do you see such examples in your own life?

3. Language can be used to bring people together or to drive them apart! How can language as we use it be either a bridge or a barrier? Discuss examples.

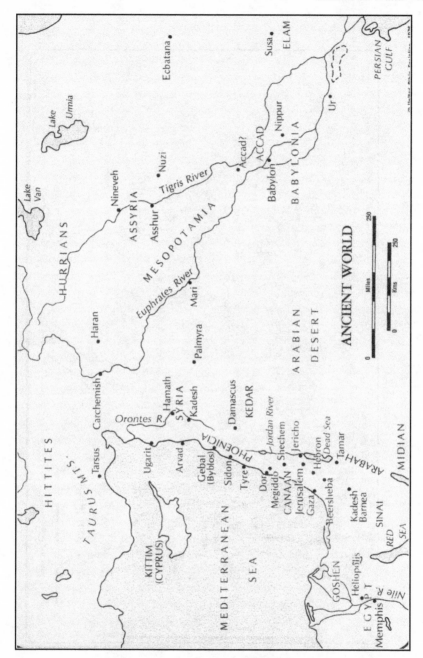

Ancient World Map

Good News Bible Today's English Version—Second Edition ©1992, p. 1533.
Maps © United Bible Societies, 1976, 1978. All rights reserved.

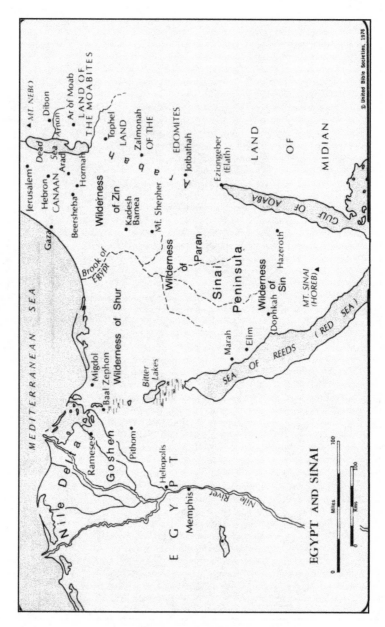

Egypt and Sinzi

Good News Bible Today's English Version—Second Edition
©1992, p. 1533. Maps © United Bible Societies, 1976, 1978.
All rights reserved.

Chapter 12. Abram's Journeys (Genesis 12-13)

Background

The first eleven chapters of Genesis describe the creation stories and the stories of prehistoric times: Cain and Abel, Noah and the Flood, and the Tower of Babel. The remaining chapters describe the Israelite patriarchs (the respected founders of the Israelites: Abraham, Isaac, and Jacob) and Joseph.

With the story of Abram (who is later called Abraham), we witness the beginning of organized monotheism. Three world religions trace their roots back to Abraham: Judaism, Christianity, and Islam.

The prehistoric Bible stories discussed the one God through short, simple stories without any ongoing relationship to God or specific expectations. The subsequent Bible stories describe an ongoing relationship with God and specific expectations.

The stories of the Israelite patriarchs occur during historic times, (i.e., during the period of writing). They were initially passed down by oral tradition over a period as long as 800 years beginning with Abram's account and then recorded. As is often true with matters of religion, the details are not always verifiable but accepted on faith by the various religions and churches.

Abram's monotheism developed at a time when polytheism reigned throughout much of the known world. The ancient people feared the polytheistic gods and sought to please them lest horrible things happen, such as floods, drought, pestilence, and other calamities. They tried to please the gods with offerings made to them through their priests, typically burnt sacrifices of their best animals and crops. However, Abram had a direct, personal relationship with his God who was portrayed as a loving, merciful, and just God. So, the Israelites were indeed very different. The story of Abram is also a story of his faith being tested in unimaginable ways!

Abram's Birth in Ur and Move to Haran

Abram was born in Ur, a thriving port city in southern Mesopotamia. Ur was located near the mouth of the Euphrates River on the Persian Gulf and now in the modern-day country of Iraq. Ur was a center of commerce and culture, known for its wealth, learning, and worship of the Sumerian moon god, Nanna. The Great Ziggurat of Ur was dedicated to the moon god Nanna.

When Abram was young, his father, Terah, moved the family, including Abram and his wife, Sarai, and his deceased brother's son, Lot, to Haran, 600 miles upriver to the northwest of Ur. Moving in those days was done by walking. If you were wealthy enough to own a donkey, you could tie your belongings to the animal or to poles that the animal would drag. The wheel was not yet in use for transportation. By today's standards, this was quite a trek for a family in the semi-arid lands of Mesopotamia. They probably traveled close to the shores of the river because the land was flatter; and the river was a source of water and food. They would travel through the villages and towns sprouting up on its banks.

Haran was an ancient city located at the crossroads used by trade caravans traveling between the Mediterranean and Persia and between Asia Minor (Turkey) and the Babylonian Empire in southern Mesopotamia. Haran was also on a tributary of the Euphrates River. While Abram was associated with Ur and Haran, he, like most shepherds, probably lived near the city in tents during the winter and roamed the countryside during parched summers in search of grazing land.

The Vision & Journey to Canaan

Abram's father and his brother were deceased at the time of the story when Abram was 75 years old and childless. Children were highly valued in those days. They were expected to care for their parents in old-age. They also cared for the family's flock of animals. The size of one's flock was a measure of their wealth in an era without coins or money as we know it. The more children you had, the larger the flock you could maintain. Therefore, God's promise (below) to give Abram at his age many descendants was quite astonishing.

Abram had a vision of God talking to him. "Leave your country, your relatives, and your father's home, and go to a land that I am going to show you. I will give you many descendants, and they will become a great nation. I will bless you and make your name famous." (Genesis 12:1-2) (GNT) So, Abram at the age of 75 started out for Canaan with his wife, Sarai, and his nephew, Lot, and all their possessions. Not everyone in Abram's extended family moved with him to Canaan. Later Abraham will send a servant to Haran to find a wife for his son among his relatives there.

Abram may have taken the caravan route, later known as the King's Highway and the Transjordanian Highway, which ran along the Transjordanian Mountain plateau. He traveled by foot over 400 hundred miles to Canaan which was not as developed as Haran or Ur. Where there were settlements, they were small. The Canaanites were farmers or herders of sheep and goats. Most lived in tents during this period.

When Abram arrived in the town of Shechem in Canaan, God appeared to him and said this is the country I am going to give to your descendants. Abram built an altar to God. In ancient Israelite times, altars were built of stone and used to honor a divine event or to give thanks. Typically, sacrifices of animals or crops were made on the altar.

Journey to Egypt

However, there was a famine in Canaan. It was so bad that Abram went farther south to Egypt to live there for a while. When he was about to cross the border into Egypt, he said to his wife Sarai, "You are a beautiful woman. When the Egyptians see you, they will assume that you are my wife, and so they will kill me and let you live. Tell them that you are my sister; then because of you they will let me live and treat me well."

When he crossed the border into Egypt, the Egyptians did see that his wife was beautiful. Some of the court officials saw her and told the king how beautiful she was. So, she was taken to his palace. Because of her the king treated Abram well and gave him flocks of sheep and goats, cattle, donkeys, slaves, and camels. But because the king had taken Sarai, God sent terrible diseases on him and on the people of his palace.

Then the king sent for Abram and asked him, "What have you done to me? Why didn't you tell me that she was your wife? Why did you say that she was your sister, and let me take her as my wife? Here is your wife; take her and get out!" The king gave orders to his men. So, they took Abram and put him out of the country, together with his wife and everything he owned. (Genesis 12:10-20) (GNT)

Abram & Lot

Abram, Sarai, and Lot left Egypt and returned to Canaan with everything they owned. Abram was clearly wealthy with sheep, goats, and cattle; and, he was thankful. He built an altar to thank God. Notice how ancient people credit their gods/God for the beneficial events in their lives, namely here the sparing of Abram's life in Egypt and his new wealth.

A problem developed between Abram and Lot's men tending the flocks in the Central Mountains which had been occupied by the Canaanites for some time. Most likely the Canaanites occupied the best land for farming and herding. There was not enough pasture land for the two flocks. Abram, the elder, pulled Lot aside and noted that they were relatives and their men should not be quarreling over the limited pasture land for their flocks. He proposed they separate. He gave Lot the first choice of land. Lot chose the Jordan Valley. They parted. Lot moved east. Abram stayed in the Central Mountain region of Canaan near Hebron. The rocky soil near Hebron was good for grapes, olives, figs, pomegranates, and some herding. It was sparsely populated. The Jordan Valley had a reliable water source, the Jordan River. It had fertile soil for farming and herding. It was also well populated. Clearly Lot chose the better land!

Notes

1. Notice the first of many promises that God makes to Abram in Genesis 12:2. God is going to give Abram who is childless at the age of 75 many descendants. His descendants will become a great nation. Nations were just being formed by conquering and joining cities and city-states into the world's first empires in Mesopotamia (e.g., by combining Akkad, Assyria, Babylonia) and in Egypt. God will also bless Abram and make his name famous. The Bible stories will soon evolve from one-way promises to covenants between God and his/her people with mutual obligations. In other words, conditional promises in which one party, God, agrees to do something (e.g., save the people) if the people follow God's commands.

2. The move to Haran may have been due to strife in Ur with the arrival of the Elamites from Persia around 1900 BCE. To the east were the Elamites, to the south the sea, to the west the desert. To the northwest was Haran, an ancient Sumerian trading post. (Haran means crossroads in Akkadian.)

3 The story of Abraham occurred in the 1800s BCE.

Consideration/Discussion

1. Moving can produce a wide range of feelings from positive to negative. How did you feel about moving to a new house or to a new school or new job? What were your positive and/or negative feelings? How have you changed as a person as a result of moving?

2 What would you do if you were Abram when he arrived in Egypt and told his wife, Sarai, to say she was his sister? Why? Remember: the king was known to have the husbands of beautiful women killed, and then the wives were abused by the king or his staff. If a beautiful woman did not have a husband, she was still taken and often abused by the king or his staff.

3. Debate: Did the king (Pharaoh) deserve to be punished? Did Abram act properly?

> a. The king abused his power by taking a woman, Sarai.
>
> b. Abram acted first in his own interests. Heroes are like all people: they are not perfect.
>
> c. This is a nightmare for Abram and the Pharaoh! Abram had to choose between two difficult options: his life and a lie. The Pharaoh and his court suffered terrible diseases right after he took Sarai into his court.

4. It was the custom to defer to the elder in making family decisions. In your opinion what were some of the advantages to Abram in letting his nephew have the first choice when Abram was entitled to the first choice by their customs?

Comment: There would be no more jealous feelings among Lot's tribe toward Abram's tribe regarding grazing. It would show Abram's love and respect for his nephew, especially in this culture where family members always defer to the eldest. This is also the beginning of a pattern in which God selects younger family members for key roles as a way of noting the importance of all people, not just the eldest.

5. How do you settle differences in a family constructively?

Chapter 13. Abraham's Sons (Genesis 15-21)

God's Covenant & Prediction

Abram had another vision of God promising him a great reward. God had previously promised him many descendants years ago when he was 75. Yet he is still childless.

So, Abram actually questions God what good will your reward do since Abram has no children to leave it to. Interestingly, the writers of the Old Testament not only portray their superheroes, such as Abram, in a positive light but also along with their less than admirable qualities, their very human weaknesses we all share. Here we have Abram politely talking back to God and questioning the value of God's promised reward!

In those days, the chief slave would inherit the property of his childless master at the time of the master's death. In a dream God informed Abram that his slave, Eliezer of Damascus, "will not inherit your property; your son will be your heir. Look at the sky and try to count the stars. You will have as many descendants as that." (Genesis 15:4-5) (GNT) Abram accepted the promise and placed his trust in God. God was pleased.

God also told Abram that he led Abram out of Ur to give him this land in Canaan. Once again Abram questioned God how can I know it will be mine! God instructed him to make an offering of several animals, which he did. As the sun set and Abram fell into a deep sleep, he had a disturbing dream. In it, God said that Abram's descendants will be treated poorly as slaves in a foreign land for 400 years. God will punish that nation; and, when Abram's people leave, they will take great wealth with them. God then made a covenant with Abram promising to give his descendants the land from the Egyptian border to the Euphrates River (in modern day Iraq).

Impatience, Concubine & Ishmael

Ten years have gone by without Sarai bearing a child. In accordance with the customs of the time, Sarai told Abram to try to have a child with her slave, Hagar, an Egyptian slave he received while in Egypt. He agreed and took Hagar as his concubine.

When Hagar became pregnant, she became proud and despised Sarai. After all, Hagar was bearing the all-important child that is highly cherished in their culture and needed for inheritance purposes lest the wealth pass on to Abram's head slave, Eliezer. Perhaps Hagar was feeling superior to Sarai! Sarai complained to Abram that Hagar despised her. Abram told Sarai that Hagar was her slave. She should handle Hagar as she saw fit. Unfortunately, Sarai treated Hagar so cruelly that Hagar ran away.

At a spring in the desert an angel appeared to Hagar. The angel told Hagar to return but also promised her many descendants. The angel mentioned that her son will live apart from his relatives. Abram was 86 when Hagar bore him a son named Ishmael.

The Covenant and Circumcision—Genesis 17

Abram had another vision of God making a covenant with him. God commanded him to obey God and to always do what was right. God changed his name to Abraham. He promised that Abraham will be the ancestor of many nations, that he will have many descendants, and that some of them will be kings. Although the Israelites will continue to be tempted by polytheism for many generations, the movement to monotheism was clear with this quote. "I will keep my promise to you and to your descendants in future generations as an everlasting covenant. I will be your God and the God of your descendants. I will give to you and to your descendants this land in which you are now a foreigner. The whole land of Canaan will belong to your descendants forever, and I will be their God." (Genesis 17:7-8) (GNT)

God also commanded Abraham to circumcise every Israelite male, including baby boys. This will be the physical sign of God's covenant with his people.

In addition, God changed Abraham's wife's name from Sarai to Sarah and mentioned that he/she will give Abraham a son by her. Abraham respectfully bowed down but could not help but laugh at the thought of a now 100-year-old man having a son with a 90-year-old woman. So again, he talked back to God and said, "Why not let Ishmael be my heir?" (Genesis 17:18) (GNT) However, this was never God's plan. God informed Abraham that he will have son to be named Isaac and that God will keep his covenant through him. Isaac will be the father of twelve princes who will later be known as the leaders of the twelve tribes of Israel. God also promised to give Ishmael many children. Abraham obeyed God and circumcised Ishmael and all the other males.

Comment: This is God's first two-party covenant, a solemn promise between God and his people with mutual obligations. That is, "I will be your God." (Your belief in monotheism). (In return,) "I will give you and your descendants this land." Previously, God made promises with little in the way of specific expectations in return.

Hospitality, a Prediction, and Another Promise by God of a Son

Opening question: How might a tribe or villager help a traveler in ancient times? In a semi-arid land without our modern conveniences such as hotels, restaurants, and stores?

One day Abraham was sitting at the entrance to his tent during the hottest part of day when he saw three men approaching. Hospitality, the offering even to strangers of a friendly and generous reception, was widely practiced among ancient peoples. Travelers were especially dependent on the hospitality of strangers they passed during the long distances between towns. People traveled by foot on dusty, dirt paths. They often needed water, food, and shelter during their journey. Abraham jumped up and invited the three total strangers to stop. He gave them a place to rest under the shade of a nearby tree. He washed their dusty feet. He offered them food to replenish their strength.

Part of hospitality was to be gracious with your best offerings. Abraham asked Sarah to bake some bread with her best flour. Abraham picked a tender, fat calf for his servant to slaughter and cook. Then Abraham set out under the shade of a tree, milk, cream, bread, and meat for the travelers who were thankful.

Hospitality, the providing of water, food, and shelter, is a custom still practiced in some societies even for strangers. It addresses basic human needs. It also expresses a basic human desire to help those less fortunate.

One of the travelers told Abraham that when he returns in nine months Sarah will have a son. Sarah overheard the conversation and laughed. How could she have a child? She was too old to have children. However, God pulled Abraham aside and questioned Sarah's laughter and whether anything was too hard for God to do. He reaffirmed that Sarah will have a son in nine months.

A Second Son: Isaac Complicates Life for Ishmael & Hagar

As promised, nine months later Sarah had a boy named Isaac which means "one who laughs" in Hebrew. On the eighth day Isaac was circumcised. Among Jewish people circumcisions are still performed at about this age. Years later, Sarah told Abraham to send Ishmael and his mother, Hagar, away. Sarah did not want Ishmael to inherit Abraham's wealth. If Ishmael was not present, he would not inherit. Abraham was quite troubled by her request to send his first-born son away. However, God told Abraham to go ahead as Sarah requested because it was God's plan that Abraham's descendants would be through Isaac, the son God promised. God also mentioned that he would take care of Ishmael. Abraham did as instructed. He gave Hagar food and a leather bag full of water and sent them away.

Notes

1. The belief in one God is not a clear concept in Abram's time but will be by the time of Moses in the Book of Exodus. Perhaps the Israelites thought of Abram's God as a God above the other gods.

2. In ancient times when a woman was unable to bear children, a husband had three choices: He could do nothing. He could divorce his wife and return the dowry he had received (as noted in the Babylonian Code of Hammurabi and other ancient texts). (Women did not receive a paternal inheritance but did take a dowry from her father to her new husband.) Or it was common for a man to have a child with a concubine.

3. According to the customs of the time, Ishmael was raised by Abram and Sarai. Although Ishmael was the child of a slave concubine, Hagar, he legally belonged to Abram and Sarai. Ishmael would thus inherit Abram's wealth.

4. Polygamy was practiced in many ancient cultures including among the patriarchs of Israel. Childbirth was dangerous for women. Many women died giving birth. And many infants died during infancy due to childhood diseases now largely controlled in the developed world. Polygamy was a way to ensure sufficient children to care for the herd and for the crops. In addition, it would provide children to care for adults as they aged.

5. The practice of circumcision originated before Abraham with the Egyptians and the Sumerians. Over one-third of today's males are estimated to be circumcised. It is most widely practiced among Jews and Muslims, especially in the Middle East. About 75% of Americans (more so for whites and less so for blacks with numbers declining for both) are circumcised. It is rarely practiced in Europe, Latin America, most of Asia, and in parts of sub-Sahara Africa. Overall rates have been declining as medical organizations around the world note it is not needed for medical reasons. However, the World Health Organization has recommended it in sub-Sahara Africa because of evidence of lower HIV prevalence among circumcised males.

6. The Book of Genesis uses El or Elohim for God or the Lord. In the nearby Ugarite area El was the supreme god of the gods. However, Abraham's God is the only God who deals directly with humans. Beginning with the Book of Exodus (Moses) God will be referred to as YHWH or Yahweh.

Commentary

1. This story is an example of testing faith and trust. Abraham and Sarah grew impatient waiting all those years for God's promised son and took matters into their own hands. While we cannot verify their age or the number of years they waited or if the author took literary license and exaggerated the age and numbers to emphasize a point, the universally accepted message here is the need to be faithful. Abraham and Sarah, in effect, messed things up by not waiting. God provided a solution that took care of the situation they created. He ensured Hagar and Ishmael's well-being and provided Ishmael with the cherished, many descendants. It should be noted that Islam traces its roots to Abraham through Ishmael and that they have their version of this story.

2. Islamic custom views God as protecting the lineage of both sons, with Ishmael as the ancestor of the Arab people and Isaac as the ancestor of the Jews and Christians.

3. This is an unbelievable story in which a father disowns his son and sends the son and his mother off on their own into the desert to find their way to another tribe. It is difficult for any parent to accept such a story and, especially so, as a divinely inspired one. However much, if any, literary license was used by the author hundreds of years later when writing the story for the first time, the author was certainly successful in getting the reader's attention and making the point about faithfulness (to God's commands).

Consideration/Discussion

1. This story is a one of numerous Bible stories about the testing of one's faith. Sarai and Abram grew impatient waiting for God to fulfill his/her promise of giving them a child. How do you handle the testing of your belief in someone?

2. Consider the problems with polygamy. Abram decides to have a child by a woman who is not his wife. What are the expectations that spouses have of each other? Why do they expect each other to be faithful? What problems may occur if they are not faithful to each other? Evaluate how spouses need to be there "for each other for better or for worse." Note the potential for jealousy and disputes if the relationship involves three or more at one time!

Chapter 14. Abraham's Sons (Genesis 22)

Years later God tested Abraham's faithfulness by instructing him to take Isaac to a mountain in Moriah and offer him as a sacrifice. Abraham cut some wood, loaded his donkey, and set out for Moriah, about a three-day journey. At the foot of the mountain Abraham unloaded the donkey and had Isaac carry the wood up the mountain while Abraham carried a knife and some hot coals to start a fire.

At the top of the mountain Abraham built an altar with stones, placed wood on the altar, tied up his son, and placed him on the altar. As Abraham picked up his knife, an angel called out, "Abraham, don't hurt the boy or do anything to him. Now I know that you honor and obey God because you have not kept back your only son from him." (Genesis 22:12) (GNT)

Again Abraham was promised "as many descendants as there are stars in the sky or grains of sand along the seashore." (Genesis 22:17) (GNT) Abraham saw a ram stuck in a bush, caught it, and offered it as a sacrifice instead. Abraham and Isaac returned to Beersheba where they lived.

Notes

1. In the ancient world the first crops and the first-born animals were sometimes sacrificed to win favor from the gods. Even in Canaan desperate parents in times of severe drought might sacrifice their first-born child in seeking relief from the gods so the rest of the family could survive.

2.   This is the beginning of a big shift from the polytheistic religions of the leading, nearby civilizations of the time, Egypt and Mesopotamia, whose gods were selfish, mean spirits in need of appeasement lest they destroy crops and animals to a single, loving God who was moralistic.

3.   Three major, monotheistic religions, Judaism, Christianity, and Islam, trace their roots to Abraham. In Islam, Ishmael becomes the precursor of many Arab people. His sons' names appear as the names of Arab tribes. Later in Genesis a caravan of Ishmaelites carry Joseph off as a slave to Egypt. Muslim tradition continues the story of Hagar (Hajar) accompanying Abraham (Ibrahim) and their son Ishmael (Ishmail) on their journey into the desert. The Jews see Abraham as a forefather of the Israelites and the man of God's first covenant with people. Christians see a parallel in Abraham's willingness to sacrifice his son, Isaac, with God's sacrifice of his son, Jesus. Muslims respect Abraham as the first man who submits himself to God.

4.   Abraham's death at the age of 175 (Genesis 25:7-8) is thought to be a common exaggeration or literary technique to underscore how wise and blessed he was.

Commentary

1.   Abraham's faithfulness was rewarded with the usual promise of many descendants.

2.   This unbelievable story is often seen as a sign of testing, a sign of faithfulness in the most difficult circumstances.

3.   Some see this story as a symbol of God's prohibition of human sacrifice. It occurred at a time when sacrifices of animals (and to some degree crops) to the gods and the Israelites' God were common. Human

sacrifices were also occasionally made in the Canaanite area of the world. God's prohibition of human sacrifice may be seen as a distinguishing factor from such polytheistic practices. It shows God as a loving God as opposed to the selfish gods whom polytheists feared.

Consideration/Discussion

1. God tested Abraham. How have you been tested in your daily life? What precious person or thing was at risk in the actions you took?

2. Reflection: Think of the difficult decisions leaders have made.

    a. Lincoln—pursuing the Civil War with over 600,000 deaths.

    b. Truman—unleashing the atomic bomb on Nagasaki and Hiroshima, Japan, during WWII which caused between 125,000 and 225,000 deaths within the first four months, half occurred on the first day.

    c. Gandhi—facing the British Empire in seeking independence for India through non-violence while being beaten and jailed.

    d. Martin Luther King, Jr.—in using non-violence in seeking for equality while being beaten and jailed.

Chapter 15. Isaac (Genesis 24)

Finding Isaac a Wife While Living in Polytheistic Canaan

Abraham settled in Canaan's Central Mountains village of Beersheba. When he was old and a widow, he had his oldest servant, who was in charge of everything Abraham owned, make a vow. He asked the servant to promise to find a wife for Isaac but not among the people of Canaan who were polytheistic. Instead the servant was to find a wife for Isaac among Abraham's relatives in Haran, Mesopotamia. This will be an arranged marriage to ensure Isaac's faithfulness to their one God.

After a journey of 400 miles and several days, the servant and his men and their ten camels arrived at a well outside Haran in the late afternoon when the women were coming to fetch water. A young beautiful woman named Rebecca arrived with a water jar on her shoulder. She was also the daughter of the son of Abraham's brother. The servant, who must have looked tired and thirsty from his journey, asked Rebecca for a drink of water from her jar. She not only gave him a drink but also filled the trough with water for his camels.

Impressed with her hospitality and beauty, the servant then inquired about who her father was. Feeling relieved that he had found Abraham's relatives, the servant asked if there might be room in her father's house for his men and him to spend the night. Rebecca replied that there was a place for them. She then ran home and told the story of her meeting the visitors from Canaan.

Rebecca's brother, Laban, returned to the well and invited the men to come to their house. Laban unloaded the camels and gave them fodder to eat. He brought water for Abraham's servant and his men to wash their dusty feet. Then he brought them food as was customary in ancient times.

However, the servant insisted on explaining himself first. He told Laban about Abraham, his wife, Sarah, and God, and how God had made Abraham a rich man. The servant went on to explain how Abraham instructed him to find a wife for his son, Isaac, among his relatives. Laban and his (and Rebecca's) father listened and decided three things. First, this was a matter involving God. Second, they agreed to the arranged marriage proposal. Third, they subsequently decided that Rebecca should be asked if she wanted to go with the servant to meet and marry Isaac. She did want to go and left with the servant.

Early one evening as they were traveling in southern Canaan near Isaac's place, they saw a young man walking in the fields. Rebecca asked the servant who he was. Upon being told he was the servant's master, Isaac, Rebecca covered her face with her scarf. The servant greeted Isaac and told him everything. Then Isaac brought Rebecca into the tent that his mother Sarah had lived in, and she became his wife. Isaac loved Rebecca, and so he was comforted for the loss of his mother. (Genesis 24:67) (GNT)

Later Abraham passed away at the age of 175. His unbelievable age is a common exaggeration that was used in Bible stories. In this case it may have been used to note that Abraham was wise and blessed.

Notes

1 As noted in several Bible references, it was common to marry within the extended family or clan. Marriage with foreigners was discouraged for fear of spreading polytheistic beliefs and worshipping the gods.

2. Although the Bible mentions the use of camels several times starting with this story, it is doubtful that camels were in use during Abraham's

time. However, camels were commonly in use at the time the Book of Genesis was written hundreds of years later. They most likely used donkeys at the time of this story. Archaeologists have concluded that domesticated camels arrived there about 1,200 BCE. Abraham lived before then, about 1800 BCE.

Commentary

Notice the hospitality, deference, and respect shown in this story.

Consideration/Discussion

1. Why do you think hospitality was so important in ancient times?

2. How do you show hospitality?

Chapter 16. Jacob & Esau (Genesis 25-27)

Isaac & Rebecca

Rebecca became Isaac's wife when he was forty years old. Isaac loved Rebecca. Several years after Isaac married Rebecca, they discovered that she was unable to have children. Isaac prayed to God for children. Then, Rebecca became pregnant with twins!

Isaac & Rebecca's Twins

While Rebecca was carrying the twins, they struggled against each other. Rebecca asked God why this was happening. God said to her, "Two nations are within you. You will give birth to two rival peoples. One will be stronger than the other. The older will serve the younger." (Genesis 25:23) (GNT) When she gave birth, the first twin born was reddish and very hairy. She named him, Esau, which coincidentally sounds like hairy in Hebrew. The second one was born while holding onto the heel of Esau. She named him, Jacob, which sounds like the Hebrew for heel.

The boys were very different. Esau was an outdoorsman who enjoyed hunting with his father. Jacob was his mother's favorite. He was quiet and preferred to stay at home. Most likely he was a shepherd who stayed close to home. According to the custom of the time, the first-born son, Esau, was entitled to a double share of the inheritance as his birthright. One day while Jacob was cooking some hearty lentil soup, Esau came home tired and hungry after a long day hunting. He told Jacob to give him some lentil soup. However, Jacob saw an opportunity and agreed providing Esau gave Jacob his birthrights. Esau who felt like death from his exhaustion and hunger readily agreed, noting what good are birthrights if I do not soon get something to eat.

Note: While Jacob obtained Esau's birthright, he still needed his father's blessing to seal the transaction. In addition, the blessings include a prediction of the future!

Deception Planned

Later when Isaac was old, blind, and nearing death, he asked Esau to hunt and kill a wild animal and then cook it the way he liked. He told Esau that he would give Esau his final blessing. Meanwhile, Rebecca overheard them and called for Jacob. They plotted to steal Isaac's final blessing! She instructed Jacob to select two young, fat goats from their flock so she could cook them as Isaac liked. Then Jacob could take it to Isaac while pretending to be Esau and receive Isaac's final blessing.

However, Jacob protested that his father would know as soon as he touched him. Esau was hairy. Jacob had smooth skin. Jacob noted that if he deceives his father, he will bring a curse on himself. But his mother told him to let the curse fall on her. Jacob got the goats, and his mother cooked the food as his father liked. She took Esau's best clothes and put them on Jacob. She put a goat's skin on his smooth arms and gave him the goat meat and some bread she had also baked. Jacob went to his father.

Isaac asked which son he was and how did he find the meat so quickly. Jacob replied that he was Esau and that God helped him find the meat. Isaac may have been a bit perplexed. He asked his son to come closer, so he could touch him. Isaac noted that his son sounded like Jacob but felt hairy like Esau. As he was about to give his blessing, he asked if his son was really Esau. Jacob confirmed that he was really Esau. His father began to eat the meal his son brought. His father kissed him, commented on how he smelled like the fields, and gave his blessing. "May God give you dew from heaven and make your fields fertile! May he give you plenty of grain and wine! May nations be your servants, and may peoples bow down before you. May you rule over your relatives…" (Genesis 27: 28-29) (GNT)

Deception Uncovered

After Jacob left, Esau arrived with the food he had cooked. His father asked who he was! When Esau identified himself, Isaac trembled. He said he had been deceived by Jacob. Isaac had already given his final blessing and that it was his brother's forever. Esau cried out bitterly and asked for his blessing also. But there was nothing further his father could do; the blessing had been given. Esau hated Jacob for he had cheated Esau out of his rights as the first-born and then stole his father's blessing. He decided to kill Jacob after his father died.

When Rebecca learned of Esau's plan, she sent Jacob to stay with her brother, Laban, in Haran until Esau's anger cooled down. She also wanted him to find a wife among her family and not among one of the local, polytheistic, Canaanite women. Esau had previously married two Canaanite women to his parents' dismay.

Notes

In ancient Israel marriages often occurred within the extended family: cousins marrying cousins. This was considered preferable to marriage to a foreigner but that, too, occasionally happened (e.g., Esau and in the Book of Ruth).

Commentary

1. Notice the theme of married women who are unable to have children repeated in Old Testament stories: First with Abraham and Sarah and now with Isaac and Rebecca. It will be continued in future sto-

ries, symbolizing the importance of children, large families, and faith in God.

2. God is changing the order of things. By rights the oldest son should succeed his father. However, a new theme emerges: The less privileged are important, too. Watch for this pattern in the upcoming Bible stories.

Consideration/Discussion

1. How would you feel if you were Esau? Jacob?

2 How do you feel about the birthright system? In some European cultures up until the last couple of hundred years ago the oldest son receive all the land. Sometimes the family property was too small to support more than one family. Does that make it right? How should a parents' property and money be distributed to their children? How would you want inheritance handled in your family?

3. How do you feel when you try to get an answer on a test from someone? Or when you get something that does not belong to you? Have there been times you did not tell the truth? How did you feel at the time? Later?

Chapter 17. Jacob (Genesis 28-33)

Jacob's Dream: A Stairway to Heaven

Jacob left home to escape Esau's raging threat to kill him and to follow his mother's request to go to Haran to marry one of his Uncle Laban's daughters instead of marrying one of the local Canaanite women.

At sunset, he camped and fell asleep. Perhaps he was nervous, all alone on a long journey, and lying out in the open under the sky after a horrific fight with his brother. In his sleep, he dreamt of a stairway (or ladder) from earth to heaven with angels moving up and down. He also dreamt that God stood next to him and promised, "I will give to you and your descendants this land on which you are lying. They will be as numerous as the specks of dust on earth...I will be with you and protect you..." (Genesis 28:13-15) (GNT) He woke up terrified. The next morning, he set a memorial stone where he had slept and named the place Bethel, which is Hebrew for house of God. Jacob also made a vow that he would worship the one God and give God a tithe (a tenth) of everything he receives if he has a safe journey.

Jacob Meets Rachel

Jacob continued onto Haran and met Rachel at a well while she was herding her father's flock. They talked; and, Jacob fell in love with Rachel. Then Jacob met Laban, Rachel's father. It was customary for the groom to offer the bride's parents a substantial gift to obtain their permission to marry their daughter. In some cultures, the parents held the gift in case the marriage failed. The daughter and her family would then have some resources to support her. Since Jacob arrived in Haran with nothing, he offered to work seven years for Laban if he would let Jacob marry Rachel. Laban agreed.

Jacob Is Deceived!

On the wedding night, Laban substituted his heavily veiled, oldest daughter, Leah, for Rachel. Jacob did not discover the trick until after the wedding.

You can imagine how furious Jacob was when he pulled back his new bride's veil and discovered he had just married the wrong daughter! When confronted, Laban explained that it was customary to give the oldest daughter in marriage first. He told Jacob that he could also marry Rachel in exchange for another seven years of hard work. Jacob loved Rachel so much that he agreed. Within a few weeks he had a second wife, Rachel, but also an obligation to work seven more years for Laban.

Jacob had ten children with his wife, Leah, her servant, and with Rachael's servant. However, Rachel was unable to have children. Finally, God answered Rachel's prayer, and Jacob had an eleventh son, Joseph, by the woman, Rachel, he always loved. Later she had a second son, Benjamin. The twelve sons would later be known as the heads of the twelve tribes of Israel.

Jacob Leaves Laban

After another six years of working for Laban in exchange for part of his flock, Jacob decided that it was now time to return to his homeland that he had left some 20 years ago. He had made himself rich partly at Laban's expense through a cunning plan to build a flock of sheep and partly through his own wise management of Laban's flock. (Jacob's selective breeding of sheep built up his herd and comparatively weakened Laban's.) Because of his deception, Jacob left hastily and in secret.

Laban eventually caught up with Jacob and sought to reclaim some missing household goods, including a few idols that Rachel had taken with her. But God appeared in a dream to Laban and warned him not to harm Jacob. Laban made a non-aggression pact with Jacob. It decided the borders between their lands. They parted peacefully and respectfully resolving their issues.

Jacob Heads Home to Canaan

As Jacob approached his homeland, he worried about his brother, Esau, and how he had treated him in trading for the birthright and stealing his father's blessing and how Esau said he would kill Jacob. Jacob wanted to reconcile with his brother. He sent messengers ahead to tell Esau that he was coming as his obedient servant. The messengers reported that Esau was on his way with 400 hundred men. Jacob was frightened and prayed to God.

Jacob Wrestles

The next morning Jacob chose a gift from his livestock to send to Esau. He had several servants take a flock of animals to Esau as a peace offering: over 200 goats, over 200 sheep, 30 camels, 50 cows, and 30 donkeys. He instructed his servants to tell Esau that Jacob "sends them as a present to his master Esau. Jacob himself is right behind us." (Genesis 32:18) (GNT)

That night he had a fitful sleep. Perhaps Jacob was anxious about meeting Esau, the brother he deceived, the brother who vowed to kill him. Jacob dreamt that he had a fight with a man. They struggled until just before daybreak. The man hit Jacob's hip and threw it out of joint. He now walked with a limp. Finally, the man asked Jacob for his name. When he replied, "Jacob," the man said, "Your name will no longer be Jacob. You have struggled with God and with men, and you have won; so, your name will be Israel." (Gen 32:28) (GNT) In Hebrew Israel sounds like one who struggles with God.

As Jacob saw Esau and his 400 men approaching, Jacob ran ahead and bowed down to the ground seven times in front of Esau. "But Esau ran to meet him, threw his hands around him, and kissed him. They were both crying." (Genesis 33:4) (GNT) And so peace was restored between the brothers. Jacob returned safely. He had his family give up the idols some had brought from Haran and built an altar to honor his one God. Rachel, his true love, gave birth to a second son, Benjamin. However, it appeared that the stress of the journey, her pregnancy, and the childbirth were too much. Rachel died.

Notes

1. The concept of a stairway to heaven appeared in the Mesopotamian culture of both the Sumerians and Babylonians in their step pyramids (ziggurats) which looked like a stairway to heaven with a temple on top used by the priest to make offerings to the gods above.

2. Jacob decided to give God one-tenth of everything he received. This is called tithing. Several churches today practice tithing whereby their members agree to give the church one-tenth of their earnings.

3. In Mesopotamia the groom's family typically paid the father of the bride a gift of about 40 shekels (an ancient unit of weight) of silver. It was held by the father and used in case the marriage ended prematurely. If the groom was unable to pay, he could work for his future father-in-law in exchange. For example, shepherds were considered to be worth 10 shekels of silver a year. Rachel was exceptionally beautiful; Jacob was fleeing from Esau and without any means. Perhaps this is why Jacob worked seven years for Laban instead of the usual price equal to four years of labor.

Commentary

The theme of this story is one of sibling rivalry, deception, and reconciliation. Favoritism can hurt. Everyone makes mistakes. Forgiveness can be hard. However, the message is that forgiveness and healing are always possible. The story of Jacob is a story of positive change and reconciliation.

Consideration/Discussion

1. Jacob is depicted as a very human character with both good and bad characteristics. He is portrayed as a trickster who steals his brother's inheritance but also as a successful herder and a repentant brother.

2. Do two wrongs make it right? Jacob tricked his brother out of his inheritance in a weak moment and then stole his brother's blessing. Was it right for Laban to then trick Jacob into marrying a daughter he did not want to marry?

3. Jacob is like us in some ways: neither perfect nor all bad. Think of how he messed up and how he acted well even in trying circumstances. Think of yourself: how you messed up and how you have acted well even in trying circumstances.

4. Think of situations where you have forgiven others. And where others have forgiven you.

5. What issues do you wrestle or struggle with?

6. What do you like/dislike about Jacob?

7. What do you like/dislike about Esau?

8. How do you resolve sibling quarrels?

Chapter 18. Joseph & His Brothers (Genesis 37)

Introduction

The story of Joseph is one of the most popular Bible stories because it is a story of adventure across Canaan and Egypt, a story of unimaginable injustices among family members, a story of unbelievable fortitude in face of cruel injustice, and a story of reconciliation and true happiness. It explores sibling rivalry, jealousy, making the best of adverse situations, facing evil with goodness, and the depth of forgiveness. Although Joseph is betrayed by his brothers and others, he consistently stays true to what is right under the most trying circumstances, including slavery, false accusations, imprisonment, famine, and near absolute power.

The story of Joseph is also a successful musical dating back to 1970 and its 1982 debut on Broadway. *Joseph and the Amazing Technicolor Dreamcoat* has been produced by over 20,000 school and amateur groups.

Joseph & His Brothers

Joseph was one of Jacob's twelve sons, but he was the first son of Jacob's true love, his wife, Rachel. In other words, Joseph was Jacob's favorite son; and his brothers noticed. For example, Jacob gave Joseph a beautiful, fine, long robe with sleeves when most shepherds wore coarse, short sleeve tunics. As a young man, he and his older brothers took care of the sheep and goats. They would be gone from home days at a time moving their flocks to better pastureland. When they returned, Joseph would give his father bad reports on his brothers' doings. As a result, the brothers were not on good speaking terms with Joseph.

Once Joseph had a dream, and when he told his brothers about it, they hated him even more. He said, "Listen to the dream I had. We were all in the field trying up sheaves of wheat, when my sheaf got up and stood up straight. Yours formed a circle around mine and bowed down to it." "Do you think you are going to be a king and rule over us?" his brothers asked. So, they hated him even more because of his dream and also because of what he said about them. (Genesis 37:6-8) (GNT) And possibly because of the favoritism by their father!

Then Joseph told his brothers, "I had another dream, in which I saw the sun, the moon, and the eleven stars bowing down to me." He told the dream to his father, and his father scolded him: "What kind of dream is that? Do you think your mother, brothers, and I are going to bow down to you?" (Genesis 37:9-10) (GNT)

The Brothers Get Joseph Back

Joseph may have been a bit unaware of the extent of his brothers' feelings. When his brothers were tending to the flocks some distance away, Joseph was sent to check on them by his father. Jacob was concerned that they and the flocks were safe. When the brothers saw Joseph approaching from a distance, they said to each other, "Here comes that dreamer." (Genesis 37:19) (GNT) They decided to kill him and throw his body into one of the nearby cisterns and tell their father that he was killed by a wild animal.

However, Reuben disagreed. He convinced them not to kill Joseph but to just throw him into a dry cistern. Reuben was planning to return, save Joseph, and send him back to Jacob. When Joseph arrived, they ripped off his long robe and threw Joseph into a cistern.

Slavery

While Reuben was away, a caravan of Ishmaelite traders (descendants of Ishmael) passed by. Traders would often bring spices and cosmetics from the east to sell to the rich Egyptians. Judah told his brothers that we would not gain anything by killing their brother. Instead Judah convinced them to sell him to the Ishmaelites. The brothers agreed and sold Joseph for twenty shekels (Egyptian silver pieces).

When Reuben returned and learned what had happened to Joseph, he was upset at his brothers and concerned about what they would tell their father. They decided to tear Joseph's special robe, kill a goat, and dip the robe in the goat's blood. They told their father that a wild animal (perhaps a lion or bear which were known to exist at that time in this area) had killed Joseph. They showed him the robe. Jacob was stunned and deeply mourned his son for a very long time. His children tried to comfort him to no avail. Joseph was very special to Jacob. After all, while he was Jacob's eleventh son, he was the first son by his true love, Rachel.

Meanwhile, the Ishmaelites, also known as the Midianites from whence they were from (Midian), arrived in Egypt and sold Joseph to Potiphar, the captain of the pharaoh's palace guard. Now Joseph had to learn the language and customs of Egypt.

Notes

1. According to the Code of Hammurabi, 20 shekels was the going rate for a mature male slave. This was the cost of two years of paid labor. Canaanites used Egyptian weights of silver (shekels) as currency because coins, as we know them, were not yet in use.

2. Spices were considered luxury items used in temples and by the rich. For example, balm from the balsam tree which grew in southern Arabia was used for its medicinal purposes. Myrrh was a perfume ingredient used in oils and as incense in temples. It is the resin of the bush Commiphora myrrh, a thorn bush that grew along both coasts of the Red Sea.

3. The reference in Genesis 37:25 to a caravan of Ishmaelites traveling with their camels carrying gum, balm and myrrh appears to be only partly correct. Gum, balm, and myrrh were carried from southern Arabia to Egypt during these times. However, camels were not domesticated until approximately 1200 BCE. The time of Joseph was about 100 years earlier or more. However, when this account was written hundreds of years later, the writers may not have imagined another form of transportation. The Ishmaelite traders most likely used donkeys.

4. In addition to spices, Arab traders would sometimes have slaves to sell in Egypt. Slaves were needed for the construction of Egypt's great building projects, such as temples, palaces, and irrigation canals and as farm laborers. Slaves were acquired during military campaigns in which defeated soldiers and captured civilians were enslaved. During peacetime slaves might be acquired through raids on villages. Slaves with a better than average ability may have been assigned to the household staffs of officials.

5. The story of Joseph's journey to Egypt implies that the Ishmaelites used the coastal road, also known now as The Way of the Philistines. In the northern Sinai Peninsula, the coastal road follows a barren, desert-like landscape. Traders and their donkeys could travel no more than two days without replenishing their water sacks from oases located along the trail which were maintained by local governors who might charge a toll.

Commentary

1. When Jacob gave Joseph a beautiful, fine, long robe with sleeves when most shepherds wore coarse, short sleeve tunics, he was sending his sons a message. Joseph, one of the two youngest sons, was to be the head of the family and not the oldest as was the custom at that time.

2. Joseph was pretty annoying as a teenager in relating to his older brothers. He appears to be unaware of the impact of his statements! For example, he:

> • tells on his brothers when they fool around instead of watching the flock.

> • receives a special tunic from his father that the other brothers do not have. It has sleeves! Perhaps a colorful tunic in an era when color was precious. (We are unsure of the translation of the Hebrew word used to describe it. Many interpret it to mean multi-colored.)

> • tells of dreams in which his brothers and his parents bow down to him.

Consideration/Discussion

1. Did you ever feel one of your siblings was favored? How did that make you feel? Think also of a time when you might have been favored or at least your siblings felt you were!

2. How can you prevent or minimize rivalry in your family?

3. Imagine how Joseph might have felt sold into slavery by his brothers and then sent to a country whose language and customs he did not know.

Chapter 19. Joseph & the Wife of the Palace Guard Captain (Genesis 39)

Joseph & Potiphar's Wife

Joseph was a slave in Potiphar's house. Potiphar noticed that Joseph worked hard and was successful at the tasks assigned. As a result, Potiphar made Joseph his personal servant and put him in charge of his house and everything he owned.

After a while, Potiphar's wife noticed how handsome Joseph was and began to desire him. She actually asked him to go to bed with her! He refused and explained how his master, her husband, had trusted him and put him in charge of everything. "How could I do such an immoral thing and sin against God?" he asked. (Genesis 39:9) (GNT) Potiphar's wife continued to ask him to sleep with her, but he refused.

One day when Joseph was working alone, she caught him by his robe and tried to lead him to her bed. But he ran outside and left his robe behind. She called the other servants, held up his robe, and accused him of trying to rape her. She said that he ran away when she yelled. When her husband came home, she told him the same story. Potiphar who was furious had Joseph arrested and put in the king's prison.

As he had done as a slave, Joseph made the most of the situation. He did what was assigned as well as he could and without an attitude. The jailer noticed his good work and was pleased. Eventually the jailer put Joseph in charge of the other prisoners and made him responsible for many of the activities in the jail (similar to a trustee in some jails today).

Consideration/Discussion

1. How would you feel if you were Joseph, enslaved by his brothers and then wrongly imprisoned?

2. What would you do?

3. What qualities do you think might have helped Joseph survive slavery?

Chapter 20. Joseph Interprets Dreams & Becomes Governor of Egypt (Genesis 40-41)

Joseph Interprets Dreams

The king's wine steward and chief baker had offended the king and were imprisoned with Joseph. One night they each had a disturbing dream they did not understand. When Joseph asked why they looked so upset, they described their dreams and said that no one understood their meaning. Dreams held a prominent place in ancient Egyptian culture. They believed that the gods used dreams to predict the future. Joseph humbly noted that it is God who gives people the ability to interpret dreams. He then asked them to describe their dreams.

The wine steward told Joseph that he dreamt there was a grapevine with three branches. Leaves came out, blossoms developed, and grapes ripened. He held the king's cup, squeezed the grapes into it, and gave the cup to the king. Joseph interpreted the dream to mean that the three branches are three days. In three days, the king will free you and return you to your wine steward position. Joseph also asked the wine steward to be kind enough to mention him to the king. Perhaps the king would release him, too. After all, he had been kidnapped and then accused of a crime he did not commit.

The chief baker also told Joseph his dream of carrying three breadbaskets on his head with all kinds of baked goods for the king. The birds were eating them. Joseph told him that the three breadbaskets that he was carrying on his head represented three days. In three days, the king will execute you.

On the king's birthday three days later, the king restored the wine steward to his position and executed the chief baker just as Joseph predicted. Unfortunately, the wine steward forgot all about Joseph and his request.

A couple of years later the king of Egypt dreamt that he saw seven fat cows feeding on the grass. Then seven other skinny cows came by and ate the fat cows. Later the king had another dream of seven full heads of grain growing on one stalk. Then seven other heads of thin, scorched grain swallowed the full ones. The king sent for his magicians and wise men to interpret the dreams, but no one could.

Then the wine steward told the king that he knew a prisoner, named Joseph, who had accurately interpreted the dreams that he, the wine steward, and a baker had while imprisoned. The king immediately sent for Joseph who was cleaned up and brought to him. When complimented on his ability to interpret dreams, Joseph humbly told the king that it was God who gave interpretations. The king then shared his dream with Joseph.

Joseph told the king that the two dreams were similar. God was telling what will happen. The seven fat cows and the seven full heads of grain represent seven years of good livestock and grain. The seven thin cows and seven thin heads of grain represent seven years of severe famine. In fact, the good years will be soon forgotten as the famine devours the country.

Joseph advised the king to appoint a wise man in charge of the country and to empower him to appoint other officials, to collect a fifth of the crops during the seven years of plenty, and to store the grain in storehouses. The stored grain will serve as a reserve for use during the seven years of famine, so the people will not starve.

Joseph Is Made Governor of Egypt

The king approved Joseph's plan. He also thought he would not find a wiser man than Joseph to put in charge. So, the king appointed Joseph as his governor of Egypt, second in power only to the king himself. The king put his ring with the engraved seal on Joseph's finger, put a fine linen robe on him, and placed a gold chain around his neck. In addition, he gave Joseph a royal chariot and a guard of honor. Joseph now had all the signs of power to implement his plan.

Joseph was thirty years old. He traveled throughout Egypt, had storerooms constructed, and had one-fifth of the grain warehoused. He collected so much grain he actually stopped measuring. During the years of plenty, he married and had two sons, Manasseh and then Ephraim.

However, just as Joseph predicted, the seven years of plenty ended and the seven years of famine began. Although every other nearby country experienced severe famine, there was food in Egypt due to Joseph's planning. He opened the storehouses and sold grain to the Egyptians and to people from other countries.

Notes

1. Dreams: Nowadays we do not think of dreams as messages from the gods, but simply as random combinations of thoughts stored in our brains.

2. Background: Ancient Egypt was known to have had periodic, severe famines. The principal responsibility of the pharaoh (king) was to feed his/her people.

3. Geography: The Delta region of Egypt typically gets less than 3 mm or 1" of rain a year. Egypt's crops and livestock were sustained by the annual flooding of the Nile which regularly occurs between July and November (the flooding season). The flooding prepares the ground for the

planting season (November to March) which is followed by the very dry harvest season (March to July). In effect, these are ancient Egypt's three seasons. The seven years of plenty refer to seven years with above average flooding which permitted more land to be farmed. The seven years of drought refer to seven years with below average flooding which produced poor harvests.

4. Diet: Egypt was a major grain-producing country in the area. The two main crops, wheat and barley, were used to bake bread and brew beer. The typical Egyptian worker also ate lentils, cabbage, and occasionally fish. Only the wealthy could afford meat, such as chicken and oxen beef.

Commentary

Notice that Joseph does not take credit for interpreting dreams. He credits God. Lesson: Do not forget to give credit to those who help you! It reflects well on you and makes others appreciate you even more.

Chapter 21. Joseph's Brothers Go to Egypt & Return There with Benjamin (Genesis 42-43)

Joseph's Brothers Go to Egypt

The famine spread to Canaan and beyond. When Jacob learned there was grain in Egypt, he sent all but one of his sons there to buy some to keep them from starving. He kept Benjamin home because he was afraid that something could happen to the second and only surviving son of his true love, Rachel. At this time Joseph was selling grain to the people of Egypt and to others from all over who were suffering.

The journey would have typically taken up to a month. The brothers most likely used the Way of the Philistines (Coastal Highway).

When the brothers met the governor, they bowed down as was the custom. Although Joseph recognized them, they did not recognize Joseph who was no longer poorly dressed as the shepherd he once was. Joseph acted as if he did not know them and addressed them in the native language of Egypt through a translator. After inquiring where they were from and why they came to Egypt, Joseph accused them of being spies! They protested and explained that they were twelve brothers. One was dead; and, the youngest was home with his father.

Joseph was unmoved and continued to accuse them of being spies. He imprisoned them for three days. Then he decided to test them. To prove their innocence, he kept one of them in prison while the others were released with the order to bring Benjamin back in exchange for not killing the imprisoned brother and to prove they were telling the truth about an eleventh brother.

While they agreed, Reuben complained to his brothers that they were being paid back for their treatment of Joseph. Reuben reminded them that he had not wanted them to harm Joseph. Meanwhile, Joseph understood all that they were saying, but they did not know he understood them. He left them for a minute and cried. When he had composed himself and returned, he picked out Simeon and had him tied up in front of his brothers.

Joseph's Brothers Return to Canaan

Joseph had his staff fill his brothers' sacks with grain, secretly put their money back in their sacks, and give them food for their journey home. On the first night traveling, one of them opened his sack to get some grain for his donkey and discovered his money there. All the brothers were stricken with fear. It looked as though they had not paid for the grain, that they stole it!

When they reached Canaan, they told their father everything: how the governor accused them of being spies, how they protested and explained that one brother was dead and the youngest at home with his father, and how the governor held Simeon as a prisoner until they returned with Benjamin to prove they were not spies. When they emptied their sacks, each found that his money had been returned. The brothers and their father were stunned and afraid.

Their father said to them, "Do you want to make me lose all my children? Joseph is gone; Simeon is gone; and now you want to take away Benjamin. I am the one who suffers!" (Genesis 42:36) (GNT) Jacob refused to let Benjamin go to Egypt. He feared that, if anything would happen to Benjamin, the sorrow would kill him. Jacob could not bear to lose both sons by Rachel.

Jacob's Brothers Return to Egypt with Benjamin

Meanwhile, the famine got worse. When Jacob's family had eaten all their grain, Jacob finally told his sons to go Egypt again to buy more grain. On behalf of the brothers, Judah refused to go unless Jacob let them return with Benjamin. Judah even pledged his own life to guarantee Benjamin's safety. At last, Jacob agreed to let Benjamin go. But not without other conditions: Take our best products as a gift to the governor (e.g., honey, spices, pistachios, and almonds). Take twice as much money as you returned with and let the governor know there was a mistake. And may God cause the governor to have pity of you and return with Benjamin.

When Joseph saw his brothers return with Benjamin, he instructed his servants to take them to his house and to prepare a meal for all of them at noon. However, the brothers were worried about being attacked and being enslaved. So, at the door they told the servant that they had brought back the money they found in their sacks after their last food purchasing trip and that they had brought more money to buy more food. The servant told them not to worry and brought Simeon out to join them. After they entered the house, the servant brought them water to wash their feet. The servant also fed their donkeys. The brothers got their gifts ready to present to Joseph at noon. When Joseph appeared, they gave him their gifts and bowed down before him (as predicted in Joseph's earlier dreams). Joseph asked about the brothers' health and about their father.

When Joseph saw Benjamin, he nearly broke down. He left the room and cried. After composing himself and washing his face, he re-entered the room and began their meal. The brothers were amazed when they noticed that they had been seated in order from the oldest to the youngest!

Notes

1. Few Egyptians learned the foreign languages of their slaves. Instead the slaves had to learn the language and customs of the Egyptians.

2. Writings and wall paintings in Egyptian buildings describe Semitic people traveling to the Nile delta to buy grain.

Consideration/Discussion

How do you want this story to end?

Chapter 22. The Missing Cup and Joseph Identifies Himself (Genesis 44-45)

The Missing Cup and Joseph Identifies Himself

After their meal Joseph had his chief servant fill his brothers' sacks with food and hide each man's food money in the top of his sack. He also had his servant put his special, silver cup in Benjamin's sack. In the morning the brothers left with their donkeys and sacks of food. Before they had gone far, Joseph sent his servant after them to ask why they stole Joseph's special silver cup, the one he used for divination (using omens or magic powers to tell the future).

When the servant caught up with the brothers and confronted them, they were astonished and swore that they had done no such thing. They reminded the servant that they had returned from Canaan with the money they previously found in their sacks. Why would they steal? They said that, if any of them had the missing cup, he should be killed, and the rest of the brothers would become slaves. The servant agreed with one condition. Only the one who has the cup will be a slave; the rest are free to go. The servant carefully searched each brother's sack starting with the oldest. When he found the cup in the last sack, the youngest brother's sack, Benjamin's, the brothers tore their clothes in sorrow and returned to Joseph's house.

They bowed down before Joseph and did not know what to say. Finally, they asked how they could clear themselves. They said they were all his slaves. However, Joseph disagreed. He wanted only the one with the cup, his full brother, to stay as his slave. The rest were to return to their home in Canaan.

Judah Pleads for Benjamin

Judah began to plead with Joseph for Benjamin. Judah mentioned how Benjamin was born when his father, Jacob, was old; how Jacob had only two sons by his wife, Rachel, who was his true love; how the other son, Joseph, had been killed by a wild animal; and, how the sorrow of the loss of Benjamin would be the cause of his death at this old age. His father refused to let them return with Benjamin until they were again out of food. Still he hesitated. With great reluctance he finally agreed to let Benjamin go only after Judah pledged his own life for Benjamin's safe return home. Judah concluded by pledging his life as a slave to Joseph if only Joseph would let Benjamin return home with his brothers. Judah could not bear to see his father die in the sorrow of losing a second son.

Joseph Tells His Brothers Who He is

At this point Joseph was overcome with emotion and ordered his servants from the room. He cried and then identified himself as Joseph and inquired about his father. He pulled them closer and hugged them. He acknowledged that they had sold him into slavery in Egypt, but he held no grudge against them. Joseph credited God for sending him ahead of them to Egypt to save people's lives. They were in only the second year of what would become a seven-year famine. Joseph was now able to save his brothers and their families from this famine. Joseph again credited God for sending him to Egypt and making him the governor, the second highest official in the land.

Joseph instructed them to hurry back to Canaan, to tell their father that he is alive, and to return to Egypt with their children, grandchildren, flocks of animals, and everything they owned to live in the Goshen area of Egypt in the eastern part of the Nile Delta. He will take care of them and ensure that they survive the upcoming five years of famine. Joseph then hugged Benjamin and cried. Benjamin hugged Joseph and cried, too. Joseph hugged each of his brothers.

When the news reached the king, he, too, wanted Joseph's extended family to settle in Egypt. He gave them wagons to use for their wives and children in their return to Egypt. And food for the trip. Joseph sent his father a gift of ten donkeys loaded with the best Egyptian goods and ten donkeys loaded with food.

The brothers returned to Canaan and shared the news of Joseph with their father who was absolutely stunned. For years he had mourned his son's death. At first, he did not believe them. After the brothers told him all that Joseph had said and after Jacob saw the gifts that Joseph had sent, he got over his shock and disbelief. All he wanted to do was to go see Joseph before he died.

Commentary

1. Notice how Joseph does not get negative and blame his brothers for enslaving him. Instead he sees the good that has come from his enslavement, that he was sent ahead of his brothers to save people with his pre-famine preparations. In guerilla warfare, there is a maxim: In every disadvantage, there is an advantage. In every advantage, there is a disadvantage.

2. Think of the disadvantages in your advantages in life and vice versa.

Consideration/Discussion

1. Think about how the brothers must have felt when they learned the governor was Joseph? When Joseph showed them love and forgiveness instead of seeking revenge, what effect do you think this had on the brothers?

2. "To err is human; to forgive is divine." What does this saying mean? Why is forgiving deemed to be so special?

3. It takes a strong person to forgive; a weak one to seek revenge. Forgiving requires work: working through your hurt feelings to the point of forgiveness and moving on constructively. How do you want the future to be?

Chapter 23. Jacob's Family Moves to Egypt & Famine Strikes Harder (Genesis 46-47)

Jacob's Family Moves to Egypt & Famine Strikes Harder

Jacob's sons loaded the wagons with their children, wives, and grandchildren and headed out to Egypt along with their livestock and all their possessions. A total of sixty-six direct descendants of Jacob plus their wives moved to Egypt. At Jacob's request Judah went ahead to ask Joseph to meet them in Goshen in the eastern Nile Delta. When Joseph saw his father, he embraced him for a long time and cried. Jacob said to Joseph, "I am ready to die, now that I have seen you and know that you are still alive." (Genesis 46:30) (GNT)

Joseph told his brothers that, when they meet the king, they must tell him that they are shepherds. The king will then surely let them stay in Goshen which will be safer because the Egyptians will have nothing to do with shepherds. The Egyptians were farmers who always worried about herds eating their crops. Goshen was known as well irrigated pastureland suited for herding.

When they met the king, he heard how they were shepherds who wanted to stay in Goshen. The king not only agreed to let them stay there, but he also asked them to care for his own livestock.

The Famine Strikes Harder

The famine struck so hard that after a while the people had no money left to buy food from Joseph. First, they begged him to buy their livestock.

He agreed so they would not starve to death. Then they offered to sell their land for food. Joseph bought their land, so they could buy food. When their money ran out again, they offered themselves as his slaves, so they would be taken care of and fed. Joseph agreed. They were thankful for he saved them and their families. Joseph gave them seed to sow in their former fields and requested one-fifth of the harvest for the king. The rest they were to keep in order to feed themselves and their families.

Chapter 24. Jacob's Last Request, Blessing, and Death (Genesis 48-50)

Jacob's Last Request

The Israelites continued to live in Egypt, became successful herders, and had many children. After several years Jacob realized the time was drawing near for him to die. Jacob asked Joseph to make a vow to bury him in Canaan where Abraham and Isaac were buried. Joseph promised to do so.

Jacob's Blessing

Sometime later when Jacob was ill, Joseph brought his two sons, Manasseh and Ephraim, to see him. Joseph and his sons bowed down before Jacob whose eyesight was failing. Joseph put Jacob's left hand on Ephraim and his right hand on Manasseh, the older son. However, when Joseph was not looking, Jacob switched his hands and blessed the boys. When Joseph saw what happened, he was upset and moved his father's hand from Ephraim to Manasseh. He told his father that this was Manasseh, the older boy. His father refused, saying, "I know, son; I know. Manasseh's descendants will also become a great people. But his younger brother will be greater than he, and his descendants will become great nations." (Genesis 48:19) (GNT)

Jacob's Death

When Jacob died, Joseph broke down and cried. He had his father embalmed, a process that took forty days at that time. The Egyptians mourned Jacob for seventy days. Then many of the king's officials went with Joseph to bury Jacob in Canaan as Jacob had requested.

Brothers Reassured

After Jacob's death, the brothers worried that Joseph might still hate them for what they had done to him. They feared retribution. They sent a message to Joseph that their father had asked them to request Joseph's forgiveness for the crime they had committed in selling Joseph into slavery. Joseph cried when he read the message and sent for his brothers. They bowed down before him and announced that they would be his slaves. Joseph told them not to be afraid, that he will not put himself in the place of God and judge them, and that God had turned their evil deed into good and saved many people. "You have nothing to fear. I will take care of you and your children." (Genesis 50:21) (GNT) He reassured them with kind words that touched their hearts.

Notes

1. We have no evidence to prove that Joseph or his brothers were in Egypt. However, we know there were famines and that Semitic clans from the Near East moved to Egypt during the time of Joseph. One theory is that Joseph was in Egypt during the rule of the Hyksos in the eastern Nile delta. Its capital, Avaris, was near the border where visitors seeking grain would have entered Egypt. Few ruins remain. It was not uncommon for subsequent rulers to obliterate signs of prior rulers they resented. Perhaps this is why there is no evidence of Joseph during the reign of a foreign ruler of the eastern delta. However, Egypt and Canaan both experienced periodic droughts that caused famine.

2. Ancient Egyptians believed that bodies needed to be preserved from decaying, so they could be reunited with their spirit in the afterlife. Peas-

ants were buried in shallow graves at the edge of the desert where the hot, dry sand would naturally preserve their bodies.

3. Embalming could take up to 70 days for royalty. In Joseph's case Genesis notes that it took 40 days, still beyond the scope of burial practices of the peasants.

4. The official period of mourning declared by the king was 70 days, two days short of traditional number for a king.

Commentary

1. Notice how Jacob is changing the traditional order: Now the younger son is to be the greater! This is another example of Bible stories noting how others are important, not just the oldest son.

2. The story of Joseph is not only a story of reconciliation and forgiveness but also of personal growth. The brothers, too, demonstrate tremendous personal growth.

Consideration/Discussion

1. How did Joseph grow to be a better person?

2. How did Joseph's brothers grow to be better persons?

3. Discuss Joseph's special characteristics. Consider what are your special characteristics.

4. Joseph made the lives of his fellow citizens better during the famine. He took the lead in reconciling with his brothers and in bringing his family together again. Consider how you have made life better for others. How have you helped your family?

5 Think how your own negative experiences have turned out well.

6. What causes problems among family members? What can minimize them?

Chapter 25. *Moses' Early Life* (*Exodus 1-4*)

Introduction

Exodus is often considered a key event in the Israelites' history. It is the story of their departure from Egypt where they had been enslaved for 400 years and the story of the covenant between God and the Israelites with the Ten Commandments. Exodus means departure. The Israelites will leave for the "Promised Land" in Canaan which has often been described as the land of milk and honey. However, it is occupied by the Canaanites, the Hittites, the Ammonites, the Perizzetes, the Hivites, and the Jebusites and adjacent to the seafaring Philistines. Canaan in ancient times often referred to the area along the Mediterranean coast from the modern-day countries of Turkey to Egypt.

The Israelites Are Enslaved

Jacob, his twelve sons, their wives, and children settled in the Goshen area of Egypt and prospered. However, over time the memory of Joseph and how he saved Egypt faded. Over 400 years later a new king came to power who did not know about Joseph. He was concerned about how numerous the Israelites had become. He worried that they might join their enemy if they were attacked. To keep them from becoming even more numerous, the king assigned the Israelites to build the cities of Pithom and Ramses to serve as supply centers for Egypt. But the Israelites continued to increase in number. Next, he enslaved the Israelites, put them under cruel overseers and assigned them the hardest work: constructing buildings and working in the fields under the blazing Egyptian sun. However, the Israelites continued to increase in number.

The king told two Egyptian midwives, Shiprah and Puah, to kill the Israelite baby boys but let the baby girls live. The midwives, who were God-fearing, did not obey the king. They let the boys live. They did this at quite a risk to themselves since the king was all powerful with no legislature or court to check his actions. He could have imprisoned them or worse.

When the king asked them why they were letting the boys live, they made up a story about the Israelite women giving birth so easily that the babies were born before they got there. Meanwhile, the Israelites continued to increase in number. Then the king issued a command to all his subjects to throw every newborn Israelite boy into the Nile and let the girls live.

Moses Is Born

During this time an Israelite woman gave birth to a baby boy. She made a basket from the reeds that grew along the banks of the Nile and made it waterproof with a coating of tar. She hid her baby in the basket and wedged it among the reeds on the river bank. She assigned her older daughter, Miriam, to keep an eye on the basket from a distance. One day the king's daughter came down to the river to bathe. The princess heard the baby boy crying and felt sorry for him. She recognized the baby as one of the Israelite babies.

Miriam asked if she should get an Israelite woman to nurse the baby for her. The princess agreed. Miriam fetched the baby's own mother. The princess asked the woman to nurse the baby for her and offered to pay her. When the child was old enough, his mother returned him to the princess who adopted him. She gave him a common Egyptian name, Moses.

Moses Escapes

As an adult Moses would visit his people, the Israelites, who were forced to do hard labor as slaves. One day Moses saw an Egyptian overseer kill an Israelite. Moses looked around, saw no one watching, and killed the Egyptian. He hid the body in the desert sand. The next day he broke up a fight between two Israelite men. One of them said, "Are you going to kill me just as you killed that Egyptian?" (Exodus 2:14) Moses was afraid and realized that others knew what he had done. In fact, the Egyptian king tried to have him killed but Moses fled just in time. He went to live in Midian, in the Sinai Peninsula. There he met Zipporah, the daughter of a shepherd and a Midian priest, and married her.

Moses's Lack of Self-Confidence

One day Moses was tending to his father-in-law's flock of sheep and goats and took them across the desert to Mt. Sinai, a mountain that will become famous in future Bible stories about The Ten Commandments. There God appeared to him as a burning bush. Strangely, though, the bush never burned up. In what will become many direct contacts between the Israelite God and Moses, God said, "I have indeed heard the cry of my people (the Israelites); and, I see how the Egyptians are oppressing them. Now I am sending you to the king of Egypt so that you may lead my people out of his country." (Exodus 3:9-10) (GNT)

But Moses actually talked back to God and complained that he is "nobody. How can I go to the king and bring the Israelites out of Egypt?" (Exodus 3:11) (GNT) God promised to be with Moses and assured him that the Israelites will listen to him and that the Egyptians will respect him. Moses asked God what he should tell the Israelites if they asked what God's name is. God said to tell them that, "I am who I am… the God of their ancestors, the God of Abraham, Isaac, and Jacob." (Exodus 3:14-15) (GNT)

However, Moses had his doubts that the Israelites will listen to him. He whined and asked what he should do if they doubted him. God had him throw his walking stick on the ground. It turned into a snake. God told him to pick it up, and it turned back into a walking stick. Just in case the Israelites still did not believe Moses, God gave him a second miracle. Moses put his hand inside his robe. When he pulled it out, it looked diseased with white spots, like leprosy. He placed it back into his robe and pulled out a healthy-looking hand. In case the Israelites still did not believe Moses, God gave him a third miracle. Moses poured Nile water onto the ground, and it turned into blood.

Moses was still nervous and told God not to send him because, "I'm a poor speaker, slow and hesitant." (Exodus 4:10) (GNT) At this point God became angry and told him that his brother will accompany him to see the king. Aaron will be Moses's speaker. Moses can take the walking stick and tell Aaron to perform miracles with it.

Notes

1. Dynasty Change

The story of Joseph appears to have occurred after the invasion of Egypt by the Hyksos from Asia Minor about 1700 BCE. Eventually they were driven out by the Egyptians who proceeded to destroy the records and buildings of the Hyksos occupation. The Israelites under the Egyptian rule were most likely considered second class and did not occupy positions of power. To ward off future invasions, the Egyptians built fortifications in the eastern Nile area. The Israelites may have been a source of labor needed for the construction projects, such as the cities of Pithom and Ramses.

2. Geography of Ancient Egypt
- 96% of the area was desert.
- 99% of the people lived on the 4% of the land that is usable.
  - o Along the Nile River Valley which was about 2-20 miles wide
  - o In the Nile Delta near the Mediterranean Sea
    - ☐ 100 miles north to south; 150 miles east to west
    - ☐ Goshen, where the Israelites lived, was in the eastern delta.

- The Nile River Valley and Delta were covered with black, rich soil.
  - o The soil was replenished each year by overflow of the Nile River which rose an average of 25 feet once a year.
- The dry desert climate has preserved materials for thousands of years.

3. Moses sounds like "pull out" in Hebrew. Moses was also a common name in Egypt, meaning "begotten of."

4. The typical nursing period in the ancient world was 3-6 years at which time the baby would be weaned.

5. The Midianites were nomadic people who lived in tents in the Sinai Peninsula and the northwest Arabian Peninsula.

Commentary

1. Similarities with Moses' Birth Story. His birth story shares some similarities with an earlier story concerning Sargon, the founder of the world's first empire. Sargon was found as a baby in a wicker basket and pulled out of the river by a gardener. He went on to conquer several city-states in what later became known as Babylonia and combined them into an empire he ruled for about 55 years until 2279 BCE. Other later stories with similarities include Hercules surviving as a baby despite efforts to kill him, Oedipus left as a baby on a mountain to die, and Romulus and Remus put in a chest, thrown into the Tiber River, and saved by a river god, Tiberinus.

2. God's Name. Upon questioning by Moses, God reveals his name as Yahweh, "I am who I am." Many understand the phrase, "I am who I am," as an expression that means we humans cannot understand the

essence of God, an incomprehensible mystery. Jewish tradition forbids saying or writing the word, Yahweh. Out of reverence Jews prefer to say Lord, considered a more personal name for God. Lord is used in many English translations.

3. Worshiping Yahweh. Some scholars believe the worship of Yahweh was unknown before Moses. When they did start to worship Yahweh, they may have not seen him/her as the one and only God. This may have come later.

Consideration/Discussion

1. Could Moses have been reluctant to speak to the king because he learned the king's language as a second language? Perhaps he had an accent or limited vocabulary. Do you think he was self-conscious? What are you self-conscious about?

2. Moses experienced doubt and fear when he considered the enormity of God's request to confront the king and free the Israelites. We, as adolescents and as adults, are often overwhelmed with the responsibilities of school, social life, work, and family obligations. How do you handle your doubts and fears?

3. Discuss Negro spirituals, great American folk songs, written when they were oppressed as slaves, such as "Go Down, Moses (Let My People Go)," "Pharaoh's Army Got Drowned," and "Free at Last." Discuss the comparison of the African American experience and the Israelite experience as slaves over hundreds of years.

> *When Egypt was in Egyptland,*
> *Let my people go,*
> *Oppressed so hard they could not stand,*
> *Let my people go.*

Go down Moses
Way down in Egyptland
Tell old Pharaoh
To let my people go.

4. Did Moses do the right thing when he killed the Egyptian?

5. In the first two chapters of Exodus, several women in two separate incidents (i.e., the midwives, Shiprah and Puah, and Moses' sister and mother) demonstrate tremendous courage and nonviolent action in helping other people at the risk of their own safety. Consider their courage in the face of an all-powerful king who was known to execute subjects at will. (Ex 1:15- Ex 2:10)

6. Discuss the forms of "slavery" that exist today ranging from women and children working in sweatshops or on farms to folks working for below poverty level wages.

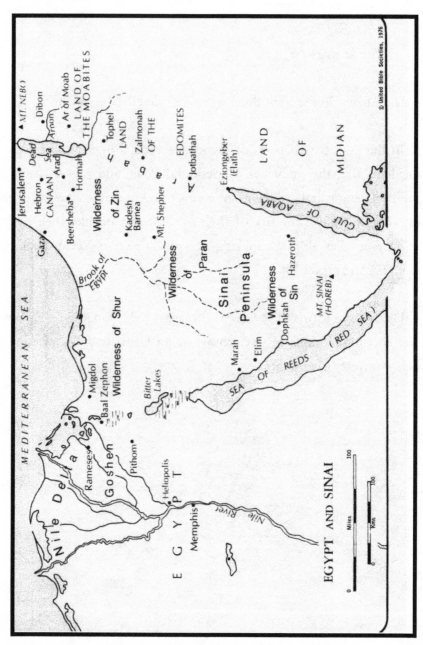

Egypt & Sinai Map

Good News Bible Today's English Version – Second Edition ©1992, p. 1534.
Maps © United Bible Societies, 1976, 1978. All rights reserved.

Chapter 26. The Ten Plagues (Exodus 4-12)

Moses Goes to Egypt

God told Moses it was now time to lead the Israelites to freedom. The Egyptians who wanted to kill him were dead. However, God also told Moses that he would make the king stubborn. The king will several times refuse to free the Israelites. In Egypt Moses and Aaron told the Israelite leaders what God had told them. Moses showed them the miracles that God had given him. The leaders believed them and bowed down when they heard they would be rescued.

Next Moses and Aaron told the king of Egypt to, "Let my people go, so they could hold a three-day festival in the desert to honor their God." The polytheistic king replied, "Who is your God? Why should I listen to him and let your people go?" (Exodus 5:1-2) (GNT) The king was upset at the prospect of losing his slaves. Who would do the work? The king may have thought that Moses was just trying to get the Israelites out of work. Instead the king commanded the Egyptian slave drivers to make them work harder. They would not have time to listen to Moses' pack of lies.

Moses Complains

The slave drivers beat the Israelite foremen and made the people work harder. The Israelite leaders complained to Moses and Aaron that they were making their life even worse than it already was. Moses, in turn, actually complained to God. "Why do you mistreat your people? Ever since

I went to the king to speak for you, he has treated them cruelly. And you have done nothing to help them!" (Exodus 5:23) (GNT)

God reminded Moses that he had made a covenant with Abraham, Isaac, and Jacob promising them the land of Canaan. God told Moses to inform the Israelites that he will rescue them and set them free. They will know that he is their one God when they are set free. Moses informed the Israelites, but they would not listen to him. Their spirit had been broken by their cruel slavery.

God then told Moses to inform the king that he must let the Israelites leave his land. However, Moses protested to God, "Even the Israelites will not listen to me, so why should the king? I am such a poor speaker." (Exodus 6:12) (GNT) God persisted with Moses. He told Moses to have Aaron speak to the king as your prophet. God has a plan. First, he will make the king stubborn. He will not listen despite numerous, terrible things that will happen. Then God will bring a severe punishment on Egypt and lead the Israelites out of slavery.

Moses & Aaron Visit the King

When Moses and Aaron visited the king again, he would not listen. Aaron threw his walking stick down, and it turned into a snake. The king called for his wise men and magicians who also threw down their walking sticks. By magic they turned into snakes. However, Aaron's stick swallowed the other snakes. As predicted, the king was stubborn and refused to listen to them.

The Ten Plagues:

Blood

God reminded Moses that the king was stubborn. He told Moses to take his walking stick and meet the king in the morning when he goes down to the Nile. Tell him, "The God of the Israelites sent me to tell you to let his people go, so they can worship him in the desert. Now, Your Majesty, our God, says that you will find out who he is by what he is going to do. Look, I am going to strike the surface of the water with this stick, and the water will be turned into blood. The fish will die, and the river will stink so much that the Egyptians will not be able to drink from it." (Exodus 7:16-18) (GNT)

Moses and Aaron confronted the king as instructed. The river turned to blood; the fish died; and, the river smelled so bad no one could drink from it. Just as predicted, the king refused to listen to Moses and Aaron. He returned to his palace.

Frogs

God told Moses to see the king again and request that he let his people go to worship God. If he refuses, tell him that frogs will cover his country, his palace, his bedroom, and all the houses of his officials and people. They will jump on everyone. The king refused. Aaron held out his walking stick, and frogs covered the country. The king called for Moses and asked him to pray to his God to remove the frogs. Moses did, and God removed the frogs. But the king was stubborn and refused to let the Israelites go.

Gnats

God next told Moses to have Aaron strike the ground with his walking stick. When he did so, the stirred-up dust turned to gnats which covered the people and their animals. The king was still stubborn and would not listen to Moses and Aaron.

Flies

God again told Moses to meet the king early the next morning as he goes down to the river. Tell him to let my people go so they can worship me. If he refuses to let them go by tomorrow, warn him that flies will descend on him and all his people the next day. As expected, the king refused, and the flies descended on all. The king called for Moses and Aaron and promised to let his people go to worship their God if the flies leave. Moses prayed to God to remove the flies, and God did. However, the king became stubborn and refused to let the Israelites go.

Death of the Animals

God told Moses to tell the king again to let his people go by the next day or he will be punished with a terrible disease that will kill all the Egyptians' animals but not the Israelites' animals. The next day all the animals of the Egyptians died but not the Israelites' animals. However, the king was stubborn and did not let the Israelites go.

Boils

God told Moses and Aaron to take a few handfuls of ashes and to throw them in the air in front of the king. As they spread out as fine dust over Egypt, they produced boils that became open sores on the people. As predicted, the king was stubborn and would not listen to them.

Hail

God next told Moses to tell the king to let his people go by the following day or Egypt will suffer its worst hailstorm ever. As the hailstorm progressed, the king sent for Moses and Aaron, admitted he was wrong, and promised to let the people go if the storm stopped. Moses prayed to God, and the storm stopped. However, the king was as stubborn as ever and refused to let the Israelites go.

Locusts

God again told Moses and Aaron to see the king and tell him: "The God of the Israelites says how much longer will you refuse me? Let my people go, so they may worship me. If you keep refusing, then I will bring locusts into your country tomorrow.... They will eat everything the

hail did not destroy." (Exodus 10:3-5) (GNT) The king tried to negoti-
ate who could go, maybe just the men. He accused Moses of plotting a
revolt. Finally, Moses and Aaron were dismissed. Moses raised his stick;
the wind blew in from the east, and the country was covered with locusts
by morning. The king called for Moses and Aaron. He admitted that he
had sinned against their God and asked Moses to pray to his God to take
away this punishment. Moses did so, and God removed the locusts with a
strong west wind. However, the king was as stubborn as ever and refused
to let the Israelites go.

Darkness

Next God instructed Moses to raise his hand toward the sky. A darkness
developed that covered Egypt for three days. The king sent for Moses
and sought relief. However, the king was as stubborn as ever and refused
to let the Israelites go. He told Moses to get out of his sight.

Death of the First-Born Announced

Then God said to Moses, "I will send only one more punishment on the
king of Egypt and his people. After that he will let you leave. In fact,
he will drive all of you out of here." (Exodus 11:1) (GNT) Moses then
said to the king, "God says at about midnight he will go through Egypt,
and every first-born son in Egypt will die...There will be a loud crying all
over Egypt, such as there has never been before or ever will be again."
(Exodus 11:4-6) (GNT) However, the king was as stubborn as ever and
refused to let the Israelites go.

The Passover

God gave Moses and Aaron instructions for the night of the death of
the first-born. Each Israelite family was to prepare a meal or share a meal
on the appointed evening. They were to kill a one-year-old male sheep
or goat, one without defects. With a sprig of hyssop (mint) they were to

put some of the blood on their doorposts or above the door's lintel. The meat was to be roasted and eaten with bitter herbs and bread made without yeast (unleavened bread). They were to eat quickly and be prepared to leave with all they need early in the morning dressed for travel. This has become known as the Passover celebration when God passed over the homes of the Israelites on the night of the death of the first-born. The blood on the doorposts was a sign for the angel of death to pass over that house.

Death of the First-Born

At midnight, the Angel of Death killed all the first-born, Egyptian sons. A loud cry went up throughout the land as a deep sorrow gripped all. That same night the king sent for Moses and Aaron and said, "Get out, you and your Israelites! Leave my country and worship your God, as you asked. Take your sheep, goats, and cattle, and leave. Also pray for a blessing for me!" (Exodus 12:31) (GNT) Over 600,000 Israelites left Egypt where they had lived for about 430 years. They took their sheep, goats, and cattle along with the unleavened bread they had baked. There was no time for other preparations.

Commentary

1. Nature-related Explanations for Nine of the Plagues.

The first nine plagues have natural causes that have occurred in northeastern Africa along with contributing strong winds. Heavy tropical rainfalls have washed red soil downstream and can create an illusion of a bloody Nile. A resulting higher than normal fish kill could cause frogs to seek land. A flood could cause an explosion in flies, gnats, and insects which could result in pestilence among the animals and infections or boils among people. In addition, anthrax spawned by the dead fish could kill the frogs and could spread among humans causing boils and related deaths. Furthermore, all this destruction could be picked up as dust by strong winds from the Sahara Desert and leave the days in darkness.

2. The Ten Plagues

The story of the ten plagues may have been intended to demonstrate the power of the God of Israel over specific gods of Egypt represented in the plagues. For example, Khnum was a fertility god associated with water (the Nile). Imhotep was a god of medicine (overpowered by the plague of boils). Seth was a god of the crops (overpowered by the plague of locusts). Osiris was the god of life (overpowered by the death of the first-born).

3. Unleavened Bread

The use of unleavened bread in Seder dinners during Passover celebrations is a reminder of the haste with which the Israelites fled slavery. Unleavened bread which has no yeast bakes quicker and does not rise. Matzo/Matzah is the name for the machine-made unleavened bread often eaten today. Unleavened bread can also be made at home using matzo meal.

Consideration/Discussion

A story of faith. Moses again and again asks the all-powerful Egyptian king to let the Israelites off work three days to worship their God. He clearly annoys the king who has the power to execute his subjects on his say so. Yet Moses repeatedly returns. Sometimes for us such faith or loyalty is difficult! Consider Moses' patience as an example of his faith. Think of your patience in faithfully helping others in trying circumstances.

Chapter 27. The Ten Commandments (Exodus 13-20 & 24)

Flight from Slavery

When the 600,000 Israelites left Egypt, God did not guide them along the shortest route to Canaan, the Coastal Highway. God was afraid that the Israelites would change their minds about freedom and return to Egypt when they saw they might have to fight. On the Coastal Highway there were several Egyptian forts that had been used in Egypt's military campaigns into Canaan. Furthermore, there were the mighty Philistines just across the border with Egypt. Instead, God sent them along a safer, roundabout way through the Sinai desert toward the Red Sea. During the day God guided them with a column of cloud. During the night he guided them with a column of fire.

Crossing the Red Sea (Sea of Reeds)

When the king of Egypt learned that the Israelites had actually left, he became upset at the loss of so many slaves. They had contributed greatly to Egypt's rise as a powerful nation by helping to feed the Egyptians and by building supply centers, such as Pithom and Ramses. He pursued them with his 600 finest chariots and caught up with them as they were camped by the Red Sea. The Israelites were terrified by the sight of 600 horse-drawn chariots racing toward them. They feared being trampled, speared, or axed to death. They were defenseless. They complained to Moses. They had walked to the desert with little food. They were tired, hungry, and now about to be slaughtered. It would have been better to stay in Egypt sheltered and fed as slaves, they complained.

Moses told his people, "Don't be afraid. Stand your ground. See what God will do to save you." (Exodus 14:13) (GNT) The column of cloud that had guided the Israelites to the shore of the Red Sea moved between the Israelites and the approaching Egyptians. As instructed by God, Moses lifted his walking stick over the sea. A strong wind sent by God pushed the water aside and dried the seabed. The Israelites crossed. As the Egyptians pursued them, the wind died, the water rose, and the chariots became stuck in the mud. As the water rose further, the Egyptians drowned. When the Israelites saw what had happened, they proclaimed their faith in their one God and in Moses. They believed again! Unfortunately, this was just one of many examples to come of the Israelites losing faith only to come back to it after a calamity.

Manna and Quails

About 45 days after leaving Egypt they came to the desert of Sin (also known as the Wilderness of Sin) in the Sinai Peninsula. They complained to Moses and Aaron, "We wish that God had left us in Egypt. There we could at least sit down and eat meat and as much other food as we wanted. But you have brought us out into this desert to starve us all to death." (Exodus 16:3) (GNT) Moses and Aaron let the people know that when they complain about them, they are really complaining about God. God had heard their complaints and told Moses that each evening they will have meat (quail, a small game bird) to eat and each morning manna (a type of bread miraculously supplied) to eat. The Israelites ate quail and manna for the next 40 years until they reached the Promised Land of Canaan.

Mount Sinai

About 60 days after leaving Egypt they came to the desert of Sinai and camped at the foot of Mt. Sinai. God called to Moses and told him,

"Now, if you obey me and keep my covenant, you will be my own people…You will be my chosen people." (Exodus 19:5) (GNT) Moses told the Israelites what God had said. They replied that they will do everything God says. Three days later God called Moses to the top of Mt. Sinai and told him the Ten Commandments.

The Ten Commandments

1. I am the Lord your God: you shall not have strange gods before me.
2. You shall not take the name of the Lord your God in vain.
3. Remember the Sabbath.
4. Honor your father and your mother.
5. You shall not kill.
6. You shall not commit adultery.
7. You shall not steal.
8. You shall not bear false witness against your neighbor.
9. You shall not covet your neighbor's wife.
10. You shall not covet your neighbor's goods.

Moses came down from Mt. Sinai and shared the Ten Commandments with the Israelites. He reminded them that they were no gods of silver or gold to be worshipped in place of the one God. It was a common practice among the polytheistic people they had lived with in Egypt to worship such an idol. Days later God called Moses back up to the top of Mt. Sinai to receive two stone tablets engraved with the Ten Commandments. Moses stayed there for forty days and nights.

The Gold Bull-Calf God

The people became restless with Moses gone so long. They told Aaron that they did not know what had happened to Moses, their leader who led them out of slavery. So, they asked Aaron to make them a god to lead them. He collected their gold earrings, melted them, poured the gold into a mold, and made a gold, bull-calf statue. Such statues were commonly worshipped by their neighbors as a symbol of a powerful god, El, who represented virility and strength. When Moses came down the mountain and saw the people worshipping the bull god, he threw the stone tablets down. They broke into many pieces. He melted the gold bull god and took Aaron and the people to task for their lack of faithfulness.

God later called Moses up to the top of Mt. Sinai and wrote his Commandments on a second stone tablet. God made a covenant with Moses to protect the Israelites. God told them to obey his/her commandments in exchange. Moses told the people all of God's commands. They said they will do everything God commands. The Israelites burned several cattle as a sacrifice in God's honor. Moses took the blood of the sacrificed cattle in bowls and threw it on the people. "This is the blood that seals the covenant which God made with you when God gave all these commandments." (Exodus 24:8) (GNT)

The Tabernacle

The Ten Commandments were kept in a special box called the Ark of the Covenant. As the Israelites moved, they carried the Ark of the Covenant with them. When they set up their camp, they kept the Ark in a special tent called the Tabernacle.

40 Years Wandering in the Desert

The Israelites continued to have weak moments of doubting and complaining about Moses, Aaron, God, and their hungry and thirsty plight in the Sinai Desert. As a result of their lack of faith, their entry into the Promised Land of Canaan was repeatedly delayed. The Israelites continued to wander about the desert for 40 years. At Meribah the Israelites were at wits end complaining what a miserable place it was without grain, figs, or water. God told Moses to gather the Israelites together, take a stick, and speak to the rock over there and water will gush out of it. Moses who appeared to be upset with the Israelites, gathered them together and said, "Listen, you rebels! Do we have to get water out of this rock for you?" (Numbers 20:10) (GNT) Instead of talking to the rock as instructed, he struck it twice and water poured forth. However, God reprimanded Moses for not having the faith to acknowledge God's role. As a result, God told Moses that he will not lead the Israelites into the Promised Land. Eventually the wanderings ended. At Mount Pisgah in Moab, east of Jericho, God showed Moses the Promised Land. Moses died, and Joshua, his trusted follower, became Moses' successor and led the Israelites into the Promised Land.

Geography Notes

1. Red Sea: The term, Red Sea, dates to a Greek translation. The Hebrew text notes the Reed Sea. Some scholars believe the crossing occurred in a marshy area near Lake Timsah or Lake Sirbonis located between the Red Sea and the Mediterranean Sea and near the Suez Canal today. Periodic, dry, gale force winds from the northeast could dry out the marshes. A shift with more moist winds from the south could restore the marshland.

2. The Desert of Sin appears to be named after a Babylonian moon god, Sin. Even before Abraham's time, the kings from the Arabian Peninsula had built a road into the Sinai Peninsula.

3. Manna: Even today manna is known among the Bedouin tribes of the Sinai Peninsula as the tamarisk tree sap extracted by insects as a sweet and sticky secretion that looks like cotton balls. When it drops to the ground, it is collected and made into wafers.

4. Diet: Bread and beer were the main staples of a slave's diet in Egypt. In the desert they would have been dependent on migratory birds, such as quail and others, who migrated from Africa to northern climates and back again.

5. Mt. Sinai is an imposing gray and pink granite mass rising 7500 feet above sea level in the southern Sinai Peninsula. It is often hidden by clouds. Local people thought of it as a home of their god.

Commentary

1. Exodus 12:37 notes that 600,000 Israelite men left plus their women and children. Could the 66 descendants of Jacob who migrated to Egypt (Genesis 46:26) have increased to 600,000 men over 430 years? To do so they would have had to double their population every 25 years which is considered possible. This would require eight surviving children per family over 430 years. While this is theoretically possible, the conditions of slavery and hard labor diminish such prospects.

Another explanation is that the Hebrew word for thousand can also be translated as clan. In other words, perhaps 600 contingents or clans left Egypt, about 6,000 men.

Perhaps the undisputed point is that a large number of Israelites left. They were not recording data as we are accustomed to do. They were writing a story passed down through hundreds of years of oral tradition and recorded in writing while they were exiled from Israel to Babylon. As some would speculate, the writers may have yearned for the more glorious days of Israel's founding.

2. The Ten Commandments

The early cities which were first found in this area were in the Sumerian part of Mesopotamia and were ruled by the priests. The functions of government and worship were handled by one person. By 3000 BCE the priests began sharing power. It was too much for priests to provide strong military leadership against periodic attacks by jealous, nearby city-states or by nomadic tribes while serving the gods. Cities began selecting temporary leaders to rule during attacks. Eventually they became full-time rulers called kings, sharing power with the priests. Kings handled earthly duties, such as organizing an army, managing irrigation canals, storing surplus grain, and settling disputes. The priests worked to please the gods who were thought to control everything. Each city had its own god who was thought to give the kings their power through their priest.

Cities were later expanded into city-states which included the city and its surrounding farmland. Later city-states were conquered and merged together. In Mesopotamia Sargon of Akkad created the world's first empire which he ruled for 55 years until 2279 BCE. A later emperor, Hammurabi, created one of the early, but not the first, organized set of laws called the code. This was an important advance that helped the king rule his empire and set uniform expectations. The Code of Hammurabi was a set of 282 laws that established behavior norms across his empire. This enabled everyone to know what was expected even if they were not near the king. It also protected people from the whims of the king! The Code was posted in each city.

The Ten Commandments arrive at a time when Moses was leading thousands of Israelites as they evolved into a nation. He was performing the duties of a priest and a king, the religious and the earthly leadership, just as others had done in this area of the world before him. The Ten Commandments and related laws that God gave Moses set forth both religious and civil law for the Israelites. At least seven ancient codes of law similar to the Ten Commandments have been found among Israel's neighbors.

In addition to the Ten Commandments, God gave Moses over 600 laws to help govern the Israelites. Many of them are similar to civil laws today (e.g., how to keep the camp clean and people healthy, how to deal with leprosy, how to handle thieves and other kinds of crimes, and how to handle issues related to marriage and inheritance).

3. Symbol of Blood. In the ancient world blood was a symbol of life. It was used to seal covenants made between kings. Moses used blood to seal the covenant between God and the Israelites.

Consideration/Discussion

1. Have you ever felt completely trapped, totally lost, or pitifully helpless as the Israelites did at the Red Sea?

2. Who provides for you? How does it feel to accept help? Do you recognize it as part of the pattern of life? To give and to receive help? Have you felt insecure like Moses or able to be helpful as Aaron?

3. Commandments/rules. Sometimes we hate rules, but could we really live without them? Think about what your life might be like with no rules. Start with your trip to school, work, shopping, church.

4. If you composed a set of commandments for your people, what would they include?

Chapter 28. Joshua (Joshua 1-6, 24)

Crossing the Jordan River

After Moses died, the God told his trusted follower, Joshua, to get the people of Israel ready and to cross the Jordan River into the Promised Land of Canaan. God instructed Joshua to be determined and confident, to be the leader of the Israelites, and to obey the laws that he gave Moses. In return, God promised to be with him and to protect the Israelites. When Joshua told the Israelites, they promised to do everything that he and God tell them to do.

God had given Moses the Ten Commandments which was now written on a scroll and kept in a special box, called the Ark of the Covenant and also known as the Covenant Box. It was fastened to the sides of two poles and carried by four men. It had become a symbol of the Israelites which was carried at the head of their marches, much like a flag was once used to lead troops into battle.

However, the Promised Land was already occupied by long-term settlers. Across the Jordan River was the walled city of Jericho. Joshua sent two spies to check out the situation. They learned that the people of Jericho had heard of their one God, how he had saved them from the Egyptians at the Red Sea, and how he helped them survive in the desert. They had seen the thousands of Israelites camped across the river. They were afraid!

After the spies reported that the people of Jericho were terrified of the Israelites, Joshua told his people to get ready to march the next day. They were to follow the priests carrying the Covenant Box to the river, but the river was high. However, as soon as the priests stepped into it as instructed by Joshua, the river stopped flowing. Upstream it backed up. Downstream to the Dead Sea the river was dry. The priests stayed in the riverbed until all had crossed. As instructed by God, Joshua had one man from each of the twelve tribes of Israel take one stone each from the riverbed and carry it to their camp that night. When the priests left the riverbed with the Covenant Box, the river resumed flowing again. That evening Joshua had the men set up a memorial with the stones to remind the Israelites what God had done that day for them. The Israelites named the place where they camped Gilgal which means circle of stones in Hebrew.

While the Israelites were camping at Gilgal, they celebrated their first Passover in the Promised Land. For the first time, they ate food locally grown in Canaan. The manna stopped arriving.

The Fall of Jericho

The gates of Jericho were barricaded. No one could get in or out. God instructed Joshua and his soldiers to follow the Covenant Box led by seven priests carrying a trumpet (perhaps a ram's horn) and march once a day for six days around Jericho. On the seventh day they were to march around the city seven times while the priests blew the trumpets. Then they would sound one long note, the people would all give up a loud shout, and the walls would come down. The next morning Joshua began following God's instructions. On the seventh day the walls of Jericho collapsed, and the Israelites captured the city on the hill. Because Joshua obeyed God, he was blessed with similar victories throughout his lifetime.

Joshua's Last Words & the Renewal of the Covenant

As Joshua was nearing the end of his life, he gathered the Israelites together at Shechem. He talked about their good fortune, their freedom from slavery, the victories they won, and the lush, bountiful land where they now lived. However, they were still tempted to worship other gods. So, Joshua said, "Decide today whom you will serve…As for my family and me, we will serve God." (Joshua 24:15) (GNT) He told them to get rid of their idols, their foreign gods. They proclaimed that they would and that they would faithfully obey their one God. However, the following Bible stories describe a roller coaster of faith, rising and falling as people struggled.

Notes

1. Trumpets date back to the Egyptians who used then to direct troop movements in battle. Egyptian trumpets were typically made of silver and bronze. Israelite trumpets were typically ram's horns, called shofar, that had been flattened and twisted into a bell shape by immersion in hot water. The ram's horn was also used for religious festivals.

2. Because archaeologists have not found conclusive evidence of an Israelite campaign to conquer Canaan under Joshua, many scholars believe the Israelites gradually settled in Canaan over time. Since there were already strong Canaanite settlements in the fertile valleys and along the coast, the Israelites first settled in the central highlands. They still had conflicts with the local tribes and also the nearby Philistines over wells, pastureland, and farmland.

Commentary

The Book of Joshua along with several subsequent books in the Bible were written about 550 BCE to explain why God's people, the Israelites, were in exile at the time. Periodically, they had lost their faith and worshipped idols. The story of Joshua reminds the Israelites of their need to turn to God as their faithful leader as Joshua had done.

Consideration/Discussion

1. It must have been intimidating for Joshua and the Israelites to consider attacking Jericho, located on a hill and surrounded by high walls and equipped with better weaponry than the former slaves had. And they must have been really surprised to learn of the inhabitants' fear of them! However, Joshua's faith in God's instructions was the key to their conquest of Jericho.

2. Some people, such as Joshua, have high standards, stay faithful to their word, and work hard. Others "go with the flow" and do not have a strong personal code. Which person is stronger in your eyes? Why?

Chapter 29. Judges (Judges 4, 6, 16)

Introduction to Judges

The Book of Judges is composed of stories between the time of Joshua's leadership and the establishment of a monarchy in Israel. After Joshua there was no strong central government. Israel was a "theocracy" (a government by officials regarded as divinely inspired) under their one God, but the twelve tribes ruled themselves independently. When the need arose, the tribes would unite behind a temporary leader called a "judge." Judges were primarily military leaders who would unite the tribes in a common defense against non-Israelite tribes in the area. Judges also provided religious leadership to restore the faith in their one God when the Israelites were tempted to worship idols. In addition, judges would fulfill the role we usually expect today, the role of resolving disputes.

Canaanite meant trader in the ancient Semitic language. The Canaanite people traded by land and by sea. They prospered. The poor tribes of Israel must have been impressed with their culture: walled and safe cities, beautiful temples, fine houses along with many small dwelling units, vases, statues, and tablets of literature from Babylon.

The temptation to worship other gods was strong. The recently freed Israelite slaves struggled with their farming efforts, especially in comparison with their more successful, polytheistic neighbors. As neighbors do, they compared farming practices. Successful Canaanite farmers encouraged their Israelite neighbors to offer sacrifices to the fertility gods, Ball and Astarte, to improve their prospects. Some Israelites may have decided to hedge their bets by worshiping both types of gods, the one Israelite God and the gods of the Canaanites, just to be safe! Some Israelites married non-Israelites and were tempted to worship their gods. Over time they forgot about their covenant with their one God.

Using oral and written sources, the Books of Joshua, Judges, the First and Second Books of Samuel, and the First and Second Books of Kings were written during the Israelites' exile in Babylon (598-538 BCE.) The exile served as a time of reflection on what went wrong. They realized that they had failed in their covenants and needed to commit themselves to their faith. The story of Joshua reminds the Israelites of their need to turn to God as their faithful leader Joshua had. Their exile was seen as a consequence of failing to follow the Ten Commandments. The Book of Judges and the subsequent books of the Bible describe the military disasters that occurred when Israel turned away from their God. The Israelites were then ruled by others. They also described the good things that happened when they were faithful.

There were twelve judges during this time. The stories of three, Deborah, Gideon, and Samson, follow.

Deborah (Judges 4)

The Israelites would periodically begin to worship other gods. The one God stopped protecting them. Another tribe or nation would attack them. The Israelites would repent and ask for God's forgiveness. God would forgive them and send a leader, a judge, to lead them temporarily in religious and military matters. This would become the cycle of the Israelites: sin, punishment, repentance, and forgiveness.

The Israelites became unfaithful again and were conquered by a Canaanite king. For twenty years he treated the Israelites cruelly. Finally, they repented and cried out for God's help. He sent Deborah to lead them as a judge. She instructed the Israelite general, Barak, to face off against the Canaanite general, Sisera. Although Barak had 10,000 men, he was afraid they would be slaughtered by the 900 horse-drawn chariots of Sisera.

Barak famously replied, "I will go if you go with me, but if you don't go with me, I won't go either." (Judges 4:8) (GNT) Deborah told him she would go but that he would not get credit for the victory. God was going to hand Sisera over to a woman. (FYI. And not to Deborah. Read on!).

The Israelites were on Mount Tabor. As Sisera approached with his chariots, Deborah told Barak to charge, God is with you. Barak's army charged downhill, and God threw Sisera's army into confusion. Although Barak successfully conquered them, Sisera slipped away on foot to the tent of Jael, a member of the Kenites who were at peace with Sisera and the Canaanites. In accordance with the customs of hospitality at the time, she provided Sisera with milk and a place to sleep. However, she was outraged that he had fled from his scattered troops. As he slept, she killed him by driving a tent peg through his skull. The subsequent "Song of Deborah" praises Jael's actions and credits her with the killing of Sisera.

Gideon (Judges 6)

For the next forty years there was peace. However, once again the Israelites began to worship other gods. God let the Midianites conquer them. Over the next seven years the Midianites took the Israelites' crops, sheep, and goats. They were devastated. They repented and asked God for forgiveness. God forgave them and sent an angel to designate a new judge to lead them.

The angel approached a farmer's son, Gideon. The angel told him that God was with him and that he was to rescue the Israelites from the Midianites. As in earlier stories our hero talks back and questions the angel. Why has God let all this happen to us? What happened to those earlier promises about the Promised Land? However, the angel persisted and told him that he will have the strength to rescue the Israelites. Much like Moses before, Gideon replied, "How can I rescue Israel? My clan is the weakest in the tribe of Manasseh, and I am the least important member of my family." (Judges 6:15) (GNT)

While the angel reassured him, Gideon, again like Moses, demanded proof! Later that day when Gideon brought an offering, the angel turned a rock into a flame to cook the meat and bread offering. Later Gideon collected the Israelites and defeated the Midianites.

After that, the Israelites said to Gideon, "Be our ruler – you and your descendants after you. You saved us from the Midianites." However, Gideon respectfully answered, "I will not be your ruler. God will be your ruler." (Judges 8:22-23) (GNT)

Samson (Judges 16)

The Israelites again strayed from their one God by worshipping the other gods. They were punished with forty years of rule by the Philistines. During this time the Israelites repented. God blessed one of the Israelites, Samson, with great strength and selected him to be a judge. Samson was known to have killed a lion allegedly with his bare hands. Over the next twenty years he killed the attacking Philistines as they looked for ways to bring him down.

Samson had a few weaknesses. The Israelites had been forbidden by God to marry non-Israelites because they would tempt the Israelites to fall away from their one God. Yet, Samson still fell in love with a Philistine woman, Delilah. Five Philistine kings kept pressuring her to find out why Samson was so strong. They offered her eleven hundred pieces of silver each. They wanted to be able to tie him up and be rid of him as a threat. She kept asking Samson to please tell her what made him so strong. Samson would make up a story. Delilah would inform the Philistines who then discovered it was false, embarrassing them and Delilah. She persisted with her questions until finally in a weak moment he told her. His strength was due to the fact that his hair had never been cut. She realized immediately that this explanation was the truth. She passed the information onto the Philistines who cut his hair as he slept and poked out his eyes, so he was blinded. They put him to work chained to a millstone and pushing the grinding millstone around and around all day.

The Philistines saw this as a victory of their pagan god, Dagon, over the God of Israel. They hosted a grand celebration. For show and entertainment, they chained Samson to two columns at the temple dedicated to Dagon. Samson repented for his ways with Delilah and asked God for his forgiveness and for the strength to avenge the Philistines. God restored Samson's strength. While chained to the columns, he pulled them together and caused the roof to collapse, killing him and more Philistines than he had ever killed before.

However, the story of the Judges ends with this famous saying: "There was no king in Israel at that time. Everyone did whatever they pleased." (Judges 21:25) (GNT) The Israelites continued to fall away from their one god and suffer more military disasters.

Notes

1. Weaponry. The Philistines had long-range composite bows made of different woods and glued together by tree sap. They far outranged traditional bows and arrows of the Israelites. The Philistines also had iron armor and chariots. The Israelites fought on foot with softer metal weapons, bronze and copper daggers and swords, and with slings and short-range bows and arrows. They may have had leather-covered wooden shields, but they did not have a battering ram to open the city gates.

2. Similarities between the Canaanite and Israelite cultures:

    a. Both had altars with four sharp projections at the corners called "horns."

    b. Both had altars for incense.

    c. Both had similar, three-part temples: a porch, a rectangular sanctuary, and an inner sanctuary which the Israelites would call the "holy of holies."

    d. Both had high expectations for their children to care for their parents on old age.

e. The prosperity of the Canaanite farming community with their religious rites and sacrifices to their gods must have offered a tempting set of beliefs to the struggling, newcomer Israelites.

3. Cycle of the Israelites

    a. Sin—idol worship (e.g., Baal and Astartes)

    b. Punishment—military defeats (e.g., by the Philistines)

    c. Repentance—Israelites request forgiveness from God

    d. Forgiveness—God's assistance (new judge appointed to lead the Israelites militarily and religiously)

4. Terminology: The term, forty years, was used here to note a round number for a generation. For example, Deborah, Gideon, Saul, David, and Solomon each ruled forty years. Forty days was used in previous stories as a period of testing or a round number for completion of a task.

5. Principal Canaanite Gods

    a. El—father of the gods and the creator of all, the highest god. He had final say in disputes among the gods but was kind and merciful. He was not involved in human affairs.

    b. Baal—the god of the storm and the day. He controlled the rainfall and the fertility of crops. He was an influence on the Israelites from the time of the Judges to the construction of the first temple by King Solomon.

    c. Astarte—goddess of fertility rites. She and Baal were considered vital to successful harvests.

Commentary

1. The story of Deborah was probably told over and over as a good feeling story of "good guys" over "bad guys" and as a story of hope that one

day the Israelites would overcome their exile in Babylon with God's help.

2. The recurring theme in the story of Gideon is that everyone is important. Gideon, the youngest child, not considered much in the family, becomes the hero rescuing the Israelites. He destroys an altar the Israelites were using to worship the Canaanite god Baal. Under God's guidance he goes on to overthrow the Midianites who had ruled over the Israelites for seven years. The least important member of the family of the least important clan becomes the hero of all the Israelites.

3. Some scholars consider the Samson story to be a folktale; others believe it as history albeit somewhat exaggerated. It was probably told around campfires when the Philistines ruled the Israelite tribes of Dan.

Consideration/Discussion

1. Samson has two characteristics: physically strong; morally weak. There are stories of him killing a lion barehanded, slaughtering Philistines, being captured, and breaking his bonds and killing more Philistines. Yet he often fell for Philistine women who betrayed him. Question: Was the story of Samson included in the Bible as an example of the good each of us can do despite our past transgressions? Did it provide hope for the exiled Israelites?

2. While we do not worship idols today, do we spend an inappropriate amount of time on some pleasures (e.g., video games, television, social media, digital devices, etc.) Do we allow them a to have an inordinate influence on our lives? (A Wind Swept over the Waters, p. 16-17)

3. Do you struggle to be true to yourself and not unrealistically beholden to others?

Chapter 30. Ruth (Ruth 1-4)

The story of Ruth is a story of a family's love during the violent times of the Judges. Elimelech lived in Bethlehem with his wife Naomi, and two sons, Mahlon and Chilion. Due to a severe drought, they moved east across the Jordan River to Moab which was inhabited by polytheistic believing people. While they were living there, Elimelech died. His two sons had married Moabite women, Orpah and Ruth. About ten years later the sons died. Naomi must have felt very lonely without her husband and sons living among different people of another faith. Fortunately, Naomi, Orpah, and Ruth were very close and comforted each other. When they heard the drought was over in Bethlehem, they all planned to move there even though the daughters-in-law were not of Naomi's faith.

As they started Naomi realized that her daughters-in-law would be better off among their own people. Each clan in those days was responsible for taking care of its own. In addition, the daughters-in-law would also have better prospects for future husbands among their own people. They all cried. Orpah kissed her mother-in-law goodbye and returned to her home. But Ruth held onto Naomi and said: "Wherever you go, I will go. Wherever you live, I will live. Your people will be my people. And your God will be my God." (Ruth 1:16) (GNT) And so they left Moab and walked to Bethlehem together with Ruth leaving her people and family behind. Ruth was determined to take care of Naomi. She even adopted Naomi's religion of monotheism.

They arrived as the barley harvest was beginning. The whole town greeted them excitedly. They were glad to see Naomi again.

One of the ways clans took care of their unfortunate members was to let the widows and others glean the fields (i.e., follow the workers and pick up any grain left behind). Ruth went out to a field that happened to be owned by Boaz who belonged to Elimelech's extended family. Boaz asked his workers who the woman was in his fields. They told him that she was the foreigner who came with Naomi to care for her. Boaz wandered out to the field and told Ruth to work with the women in this field. His workers would ensure her safety and provide water for her to drink. Ruth asked why he was so kind to a foreigner. Boaz mentioned how impressed he was that she would leave her people to care for her mother-in-law.

At mealtime Boaz joined his workers and Ruth and offered them some bread and sauce. When she returned to the field to glean, Boaz told his workers to leave behind some grain for her to pick up. At the end of the day, she had collected nearly twenty-five pounds of grain. Naomi was impressed and even more pleased when she found out that Ruth was gleaning in Boaz's field. She knew that, as his relative, he would take care of them.

The relationship between Boaz and Ruth continued to blossom. Boaz married Ruth and together they had a son, Obed. He had a son named Jesse who became the father of David, the famous David in the lineage of Jesus. And so, it came to be that Jesus had a Gentile (non-Israelite, non-Jew) in his ancestry.

Commentary

1. The Story. Although it is set in the same time period, the story of Ruth could not be more different than the stories of the Judges. It was passed down by oral tradition and written after the period of exile. Storytellers probably told the story of Ruth while visiting village festivals. The story shows how a good ending can evolve from a difficult situation and how King David, an ancestor of Jesus, had a Gentile as his great-grandmother. Ruth's concern for the survival of her mother-

in-law, Naomi, shows a strength of character that exceeds that of many other Biblical characters.

2. Gleaning. Naomi faced a tough life back home in Bethlehem. Her husband's family line had ended. Widows were not directly provided for. They could glean fields and fend for themselves. Gleaning was not theft nor begging. According to Israelite law, gleanings should be left for the poor: "Do not grain at the edges of your field and do not go back for the grain left behind. Leave them for the poor and the foreigners." (Leviticus 23:22) (GNT)

3. Marriage. It had been debated whether Gentiles would be welcome by marriage in the Jewish community. The story of Ruth, written after exile, answers that question by warmly welcoming a Moabite into that community.

4. Contrasting Summary

Judges	Ruth
• Leaders	• Hardworking Farmers
• Military Battles	• Life's Destiny
• Israelite Cycle:	• Positive Themes:
Sin	Selflessness
Punishment	Patience
Repentance	Loyalty
Forgiveness	Gentle Kindness

Consideration/Discussion

1. How does the story of Ruth challenge you?

2. Have you stuck by a friend or relative in difficult times?

3. Interview a devoted, married couple or two very close friends. Ask them about the benefits and difficulties they experienced in their commitment to each other. What makes the relationship special? What do they each contribute to it?

Chapter 31. Samuel
(1 Samuel 1-2, 8-10)

Overview of the Times

When the Israelites arrived in the Promised Land, they found it already occupied by the Canaanites who had settled in the more fertile land along the coast and in the Jordan River valley. Because the Canaanites were excellent farmers and the Israelites were not, the Israelites began to use Canaanite farming practices which included the worship of the god and goddess, Baal and Astarte. They were the fertility god and goddess who were thought to have great control over the productivity of the land and its crops.

While the Israelites began to worship other gods in addition to their one God, they appeared to have remained faithful to other Israelite cultural practices, such as avoiding pork. Archaeologists have found many pig bones in their excavations in Philistine territory but none in the Israelite highlands. This evidence shows that Israelite farmers did not raise pigs or eat pork.

Life during the Time of Judges and the Early Kings

1. Town Life. Ancient towns during this period were typically communities of 1,000-3,000 people crowded inside the city walls on top of a small hill or a tell (a mound formed by the accumulated remains of ancient settlements). The area inside the city walls was crowded with little public or open space and with many narrow, twisting alleys. The typical house was built on a stone base with mudbrick walls and a flat roof which was a

cool place to sleep in the hot weather. Israelite houses typically had four rooms built around a small courtyard: a stable for animals, a central storage area, a living space, and sleeping quarters. The house would also have cisterns that collected rainwater.

The wealthy tended to have a courtyard and a second story; the poorer people lived in smaller, crowded, one-two room blocks. The public square was often outside the main gate but in an area protected by a set of outer gates which could be raised for defense. The public square was used as a market place and a site for holding judicial-type hearings. Some of the larger towns had drains for sewage and street water. Most towns did not.

2. Sickness. Ancient people knew little about the causes of disease and death. They did use some natural remedies and some strange ones, such as animal parts. They often attributed illness and disease to evil spirits and offered prayers and sacrifices to the gods for relief. Average lifespans were thought to be in the early 40s although exceptions were common.

3. Death. There is little evidence of an Israelite belief in an afterlife until after their period in exile. Yet Israel was surrounded by civilizations believing in an afterlife (e.g., Egypt and Mesopotamia).

Introduction to the First Book of Samuel

The First Book of Samuel picks up from the closing quote in the Book of Judges: "There was no king in Israel at that time. Everyone did whatever they pleased." (Judges 21:25) (GNT) The Israelites continued to fall away from their one God and suffer more military disasters. They did not have a permanent leader to unify the twelve tribes on religious and military matters. Finally, Samuel came on the scene and was the last of the great judges and a prophet who was close to God.

The First Book of Samuel describes the transition from judges to a monarchy which involved three key people: Samuel, the last great judge and the first prophet to minister to the kings of Israel; Saul, the first king; and, David, the second king whose early life was interwoven with Saul. (The fourth great leader of this time, Solomon, is described in the next book, Kings.) The theme of the Books of Samuel and Kings is the same as earlier books: faithfulness brings success; disobedience brings military disaster. Mixed feelings about the establishment of a monarchy are noted. God was regarded as the real king of Israel. However, the people were clamoring for a king on earth, just like their neighbors had.

The fragmented, poorly armed tribes of Israel were frequently threatened by the mighty "sea people," the Philistines, who constantly pushed eastward from the coast armed with horse-drawn chariots and iron weapons. The Israelites did not have chariots. They only had weapons made with the softer metal, bronze. Each time the Israelites were attacked, the tribes had to select a leader to raise an army and pull them together as one. After the threat subsided, the Israelites acted as twelve, individual tribes again. This is the story first of survival under Saul, then success in expanding under David, and later living in prosperity and in peace under Solomon.

Another Childless Couple

There was a couple named Hannah and Elkanah who had no children. Hannah was deeply distressed. She went to the priest, Eli, and prayed to God. She promised that, if she had a son, she would dedicate him to God. She became pregnant, had a son, and named him Samuel. After weaning him, she took Samuel to the temple at Shiloh to dedicate him to God. He stayed at the temple to serve God under Eli.

Eli's own sons were scoundrels who did not follow the temple's rules. They disrespected the offerings people brought and thus insulted God. They took food offered as sacrifices when they should not have. They slept with women who worked at the entrance to the temple. They accepted bribes and did not decide cases fairly. Although Eli confronted his sons about their misdeeds, they persisted. Finally, they were both killed in battle with the Philistines on the same day which was seen as a sign of God's displeasure with them. Soon after receiving the news, Eli fell, broke his neck, and died on the same day as his sons.

Samuel

Samuel began filling the role as a priest and judge, and later as a prophet. As Samuel grew old, he made his sons judges. However, they did not follow their father's good works. Instead they accepted bribes and did not decide cases fairly. The leaders of the Israelites approached the aging Samuel to complain about the predicament they were facing. Soon Samuel's sons would become the chief judges upon Samuel's death. Instead of accepting Samuel's corrupt sons as their leaders, they requested that he appoint a king to rule them just as other countries had a king.

Request for A King

Samuel was displeased with the request and prayed to God. God said, "Listen to everything the people say to you. You are not the one they have rejected; I am the one they have rejected as their king. Ever since I brought them out of Egypt, they have turned away from me and worshiped other gods; and now they are doing to you what they have done to me. So then, listen to them but give them strict warnings and explain how their kings will treat them." (1 Samuel 8:7-9) (GNT)

Samuel told the people everything God had said to him. Samuel explained how the king will make soldiers of their sons. Some will be in chariots while others will march on foot before the chariots. Some will be officers in charge of a thousand men while others will be in charge of fifty men. Their sons will have to plow the king's fields, harvest his crops, and make his weapons and equipment. Their daughters will have to make perfumes for him (for this is in the day before daily showers or baths and deodorant). They will also have to cook for him. The king will take your best fields, olive groves, and vineyards for his use and for his officials. He will need your servants and best cattle and donkeys to work for him. He will take a tenth of your flock. You will complain bitterly about the king you chose but God will not answer your complaints.

The people were not moved and demanded that Saul anoint a king like other nations to rule them and to lead them in battle against their enemies.

A King Is Chosen

One day as Samuel was traveling among the tribes, God told him that he would send a man from the tribe of Benjamin to be anointed as king of the Israelites. When Samuel saw Saul, who was looking for his lost donkeys, God told Samuel that Saul is the man who will rule Israel. Samuel revealed God's plan to make him the king of the Israelites. Saul answered, "I belong to the tribe of Benjamin, the smallest tribe in Israel, and my family is the least important one of the tribe. Why, then, do you talk to me like this?" (1 Samuel 9:21) (GNT) Samuel explained God's plan, took olive oil, and anointed him as the king of Israel. He then called the people together to announce the chosen king. Each tribe anticipated it would be one of their own. Saul who was hiding behind the supplies had to be brought out for the announcement. The fact that he was a foot taller than anyone else helped some to accept him while others despised him.

Summary

In 1030 BCE Saul was anointed king of the Israelites due to the Israelites' fear of being ruled by Samuel's corrupt sons and due to their fear of the menacing Philistines. They may have also been jealous of the military success and the prosperity of their neighbors who all had kings. The anointment of Saul as king follows a familiar pattern: God selecting the lowest and least important. Saul is an ordinary person.

Notes

1.   During their exile from the Promised Land, the stories of the First and Second Books of Samuel were written by an unknown author about 550 BCE. The author's purpose was to describe the sins of the kings (i.e., their unfaithfulness to God) and thus explain how the Israelites came to be exiled (i.e., by suffering a military defeat as punishment for their unfaithfulness to their one God).

2.   The Books of Samuel and Kings were once presented as a single book when scrolls were used. They were divided into four books and given their current names in the Septuagint, the oldest Greek translation of the Old Testament.

3.   Note the pattern of Biblical women first having difficulty getting pregnant and then having their prayers answered: Abraham and Sarah, Isaac and Rebecca, Jacob and Rachel, Elkanah and Hannah.

4.   Samuel used olive oil to anoint Saul. Every Israelite king from then on was anointed, not crowned. The use of oil was an ancient symbol of holiness. The Hebrew word, Messiah, means "the Anointed One" as does Christ in Greek.

5.   At the time of Samuel, kings were common in large countries such as Egypt, Assyria, Babylon and among smaller neighbors such as Edom, Moab, and Ammon. Generally, their kings were thought to be divine.

Discussion/Consideration

1.   How does the following theme also apply to your life? Faithfulness brings success; disobedience brings disaster.

a.   Note how faithfulness brings order and higher productivity and standards of living to a society. However, there is also a need for creativity that may come out of chaos or freer times. While disobedience often brings disaster because it undermines the productivity of society, it is sometimes the noble course of action in matters of principle and morals. Or not!

2.   You have probably heard this: The grass is always greener on the other side of the fence. Sometimes we look at what other people have—their families, houses, possessions, appearance, and so on—and we believe our life would be better if we had what they have. But have you considered what challenges those other people face with what they have?

Chapter 32. Saul (1 Samuel 11-16)

Saul's Battles

Only one month later, the Ammonites attacked Jabesh, a small Israelite town. When Saul heard this, he felt the spirit of God and sent messengers throughout the land demanding men to lead into battle. Over 300,000 Israelites responded, some out of fear of their one God. Saul organized the men into three groups and attacked the Ammonites at dawn. By noon the Ammonites had been defeated, and the survivors scattered. Once more the Israelites proclaimed Saul as their king. The remaining doubters were impressed by Saul's actions that day. All the Israelites celebrated the victory. And Samuel reminded them of the need to remain faithful to God even though they had asked for a king.

A Weakness of Saul

Meanwhile, the Philistines were continuing their attacks on Israel at Gilgal. They had 30,000 war chariots and thousands of troops. The Israelites were trembling in fear. Some hid in caves; others moved east across the Jordan River. As instructed by Samuel, Saul awaited his arrival before attacking. In accordance with their custom, a priest would offer prayers and sacrifices to God and seek help before attacking. Only a priest could offer sacrifices. After waiting seven days for Samuel, some of the Israelites began deserting Saul. So, Saul went ahead without Samuel and offered a sacrifice to God. Just as he was finishing, Samuel arrived. He took Saul to task for not waiting as instructed. Saul protested that the people were leaving, and the Philistines were about to attack before he tried to win

God's favor. So, he felt he had to offer a sacrifice.

"That was a foolish thing to do," Samuel answered. "You have not obeyed the command God gave you. If you had obeyed, he would have let you and your descendants rule over Israel forever. But now your rule will not continue. Because you have disobeyed him, God will find the kind of man he/she wants and make him ruler of his/her people." (1Samuel 13:13-14) (GNT)

Saul's son, Jonathan, fought a daring battle against one group of Philistines and defeated them. Saul continued to battle other Philistines, and eventually they withdrew from Israel temporarily. For the remainder of his life Saul continued to fiercely and heroically fight numerous Gentile tribes, including the Philistines, Ammonites, and Moabites among others.

Another Weakness of Saul

In one war against the Amalekites Samuel instructed Saul to kill all the people and animals. Slaughtering everyone was a common practice among tribes at the time. However, in defeating the Amalekites, Saul spared the life of its king and of his best sheep and cattle. He planned to offer the animals as a sacrifice to God. However, God was not pleased that Saul did not obey his/her commands as transmitted through Samuel. When Samuel informed Saul of the God's displeasure with him, Saul protested that he was planning to use the animals in a sacrifice to God and not for his own benefit.

Samuel said, "Which does God prefer: obedience or offerings and sacrifices? It is better to obey him than to sacrifice the best sheep to him…Because you have rejected God's command, he has rejected you as king." (1 Samuel 15:22-23) (GNT) Saul owned up to his misdeed and begged forgiveness, but it was too late. The decision had been made.

David Is Anointed

God sent Samuel to Bethlehem to anoint one of Jesse's sons as the next king. Upon arriving he saw Jesse's son, Eliab, and thought this must be the one. But God said to him, "Pay no attention to how tall and handsome he is. I have rejected him, because I do not judge as people judge. They look at the outward appearance, but I look at the heart." (1Samuel 16:7) (GNT) Jesse brought out seven of his sons, one by one, but Samuel rejected them and inquired if he had any other sons. Jesse replied that his youngest son was out taking care of the sheep. Jesse sent for him. God told Samuel that this is the one to anoint. Samuel anointed David in front of his brothers. The spirit of God was now with David. However, the designation of the next king, David, was not announced to the people of Israel at this time.

Saul's Depression

When the spirit of God left Saul, he fell into a depression. His staff asked if they could find someone to play the harp for him and pick up his spirits. Saul agreed, and they sent an attendant to fetch Jesse's son David who was known as a good musician. Jesse sent David to Saul with a young goat, bread, and a leather bag full of wine. Saul liked David. Whenever Saul was down, David would play his harp and cheer up Saul.

Notes

Saul's home was in Gibeah, about three miles north of Jerusalem.

Commentary

1. Saul's downfall as a king was caused by the substitution of his own judgment in place of clear directions. Saul disobeyed God twice: First by offering a pre-battle sacrifice instead of waiting for Samuel to do it. Only priests were allowed to offer sacrifices. Second, when he captured the enemy king and his best livestock instead of killing them as instructed. As

a result, his descendants will not rule Israel. God let him finish his reign, but Saul knew he had lost the support of God. It showed in his bouts of depression and, in the next chapter, in his jealousy of Davis's accomplishments and popularity.

2. Saul's accomplishments included establishing an army, organizing the new kingdom, and defending Israel from the attacking Philistines. His success in organizing the Israelites and defending Israel paved the way for David to build on that progress and expand the kingdom. Saul reigned from approximately 1030 to 1010 BCE.

Consideration/Discussion

1. What do you think is the message in God's loss of confidence in Saul?

2. Do you think God was fair?

3. How would you describe Saul?

Chapter 33. Young David
(1 Samuel 17-31)

Goliath

The Philistines were again gathering to attack the Israelites. They were lined up on one hill and the Israelites on another with a valley between them. A tall, huge man, named Goliath, came out of the battle line wearing bronze armor and a bronze helmet and carrying a heavy bronze javelin and shield. Every morning and evening for forty days Goliath challenged the Israelites to what was known in the ancient world as single combat. To avoid widespread bloodshed, a combatant would challenge the other side to put up one combatant to fight a duel, typically until the death of one of them. The fight would occur on the open ground between the two opposing armies.

Goliath stood and shouted at the Israelites, "What are you doing there lined up for battle? I am a Philistine, you slaves of Saul. Choose one of your men to fight me. If he wins and kills me, we will be your slaves; but if I win and kill him, you will be our slaves. Here and now I challenge the Israelite army. I dare you to pick someone to fight me." When Saul and his men heard this, they were terrified. (1 Samuel 17:8-11) (GNT) This was understandable considering Goliath's size and armor.

One day Jesse sent David to the Israelite camp to bring food to his brothers who were with Saul's army. He arrived as the soldiers were lining up, and Goliath was challenging them to single combat. Some of the Israelites were running away in terror. Others were mumbling how Saul had promised a big reward to the man who would kill Goliath. He would receive the king's daughter in marriage, and Saul would free his father's family from taxes. Eliab, David's oldest brother, heard David talking to the soldiers. Although he tried to send David home, David persisted in asking the soldiers questions. Finally, he approached Saul. If no one will fight this Philistine, David said he would. Saul told him that he was just a boy and that Goliath had been a soldier all his life. But David persisted, saying that as a shepherd, he had killed lions and bears and would do the same to this heathen Philistine. God had saved him before; God will save him again. So, Saul agreed and gave David his armor, helmet, and sword. However, David was not used to wearing such armor or using such weapons. He took them off. He picked up his shepherd's stick, five smooth stones, and his sling and went to meet Goliath.

David Fights Goliath

As Goliath approached and saw David was just a boy, he cursed David and threatened to give his body to the birds to eat. But David replied that Goliath was coming with a javelin and armor while he was coming in the name of the God of the Israelite army. And that he, David, would give the bodies of the Philistine soldiers to the birds to eat. As Goliath approached, David walked toward him, reached into his bag, put a stone in his sling, and swung it toward Goliath. It hit Goliath just under his helmet on his unprotected forehead and broke his skull. The mighty Goliath fell to the ground dead. In panic the Philistines ran away, and the Israelites chased them, wounding and killing many along the way.

David returned to Saul a hero. He became a close friend of Saul's son, Jonathan, who was also a hero from his previous battle victory. David was successful on subsequent military missions. Saul made him an officer in his army. The army's officers and men were pleased.

David and Jonathan became very close friends. Jonathan shared his clothes with David. He dealt with his father's jealousy of David. Jonathan sided with David over his father. In the ultimate test of friendship, Jonathan risked his life for David.

Saul's Jealousy & David's Marriage

As Saul and David returned from the battle, the women in every town came out to greet them. They sang praises to King Saul noting he had killed thousands. They also sang praises to David noting he had killed tens of thousands. Saul became angry and then jealous of David's popularity. He thought they might make David the king. The next day Saul raved about as a madman. As David was playing his harp to cheer him up, Saul picked up a spear and threw it at David twice. Somehow David managed to dodge each one. Saul was jealous because he realized the spirit of God was with David and not him.

Saul sent David away by placing him in charge of a thousand men and sending them into battle. But God was with David. He was successful. The people loved him. Saul became even more jealous.

As promised Saul offered his oldest daughter, Merab, to David in marriage on the condition that he fight another battle. Saul thought the Philistines would kill him this time. They did not! However, when the time came for the wedding, Merab had already been given to another man. In the meantime, Saul's daughter, Michal, had fallen in love with David. Saul decided to use this as a trap. He offered Michal to David in marriage if he would first kill a hundred Philistines. Saul thought the Philistines would surely kill him this time. However, David was successful in defeating the Philistines and killing two hundred of them. He returned from the battle a hero and married Michal.

Saul Again Plans to Kill David

Saul mentioned to his son, Jonathan, that he planned to kill David. Jonathan was closer to his friend, David, than to his father. Jonathan told David of his father's intentions and warned him to be careful around his father. One day while David was playing his harp for Saul, Saul grabbed a spear and threw it at David. David ducked just in time, and the spear hit the wall. David fled the palace. That same night Saul sent men to David's house to kill him. However, Michal learned of the plan and warned him to escape before the men arrived.

David was expected to attend the upcoming New Moon Festival at the palace. Because he was afraid that Saul would kill him, he had Jonathan explain his absence as a need to visit his own family in Bethlehem for their festival. Saul immediately saw through the excuse. In anger he threw a spear at his own son accusing him of siding with David. Jonathan left the table in rage as he realized just how determined his father was to kill David.

The Hill Country

David fled to the hill country (also known as the Central Mountains) and lived in the wild occasionally getting supplies from friendly villagers. Saul went looking for David with 3,000 of his best soldiers. After one long day of searching, Saul lay down in a cave to take a nap. Coincidentally, David was hiding farther back in the same cave. He approached the sleeping Saul. David did not kill Saul out of respect for God who chose Saul as the king. Instead of killing him, David cut off a piece of his robe. When Saul awoke, he asked why David was trying to kill him. David said that you can see by the piece of your cloth that I am holding that I could have killed you. This should convince you that I have no evil intentions.

Saul started crying. "You are right, and I am wrong. You have been so good to me, while I have done such wrong to you!...How often does someone catch an enemy and then let him go away unharmed?" (1 Samuel 24:17-19) Saul acknowledged that David will become the king of Israel. He asked David to spare his descendants. David agreed.

Later when Samuel died, all the Israelites mourned for him and buried him in his hometown. Saul and his sons fought another battle against the Philistines. Many Israelites were killed, including Saul and his sons. The Israelites mourned their deaths.

Notes

1. David most likely used a sling as a shepherd against attacking animals.

2. A sling is a leather strap shaped to hold a small, round stone in the middle. It is tied at each end with a cord or thinner strap of leather. Then it is whirled about your head. One end is released with the stone hurling at up 90 miles per hour toward your target.

3. Ancient armies used contingents of slingers in battle.

4. The Philistines did not live up to their end of the deal to become slaves after the David and Goliath fight. They ran away but the Israelites wounded and killed many along the way.

5. The Philistines were the major enemy of the Israelites during the time of the Judges and the early kings, Saul and David, until they were defeated by King David about 1000 BCE. The Philistines were thought to have come from Crete in the 13th or 12th century BCE and to have settled along the coast in five city-states: Gaza, Ashkelon, Gath, Ashdod, and Ekron. Then they pushed inland toward the hill country (Central Mountains) where the Israelites had settled. The Philistines were better at open-plain battles, perhaps due to their experience and due to their use of chariots. The Israelites were more used to mounting raids from the hill country. Both used the following weapons: bows and arrows, spears (or javelins), knives, swords, and shields. The opponents lined up at an appointed time. They began fighting with a battle shout. Shield carrying soldiers led, followed by swordsmen and archers. The ensuing hand-to-hand combat con-

tinued until a victory or retreat horn was sounded. Troops returned to battle again later that day or the next.

6.   In the early days of the kingdom the Ark of the Covenant was kept in a special tent (the Tabernacle) at Shiloh. Later the ark was housed in the inner sanctuary of the Temple in Jerusalem under Solomon.

Commentary

1.   The story of David and Jonathan is a great tale of friendship and its love, loyalty, and risks. David and Jonathan were very close friends. Jonathan shared his clothes with David and dealt with his father's jealousy of David. Jonathan sided with David over his father and risked his life for David.

2.   Jealousy can destroy friendships and family relationships as we have seen with Saul and his relationship with David and Jonathan. Friendships take a lot of work to maintain through good times and bad, through moments of joy and moments of hurt feelings and doubt. Real friends do not flee when insulted but check in to find out what went wrong and to help repair the relationship. Did your friend just have a traumatic experience, such as a death in the family or other crisis which caused him or her to act out of character? Your friend might welcome your concern. For it takes two to maintain a relationship.

3.   Thoughts about jealousy:
  • Jealousy is negative; caring is positive.
  • Jealousy is destructive to you and others; love is constructive for you and others.
  • Jealousy is a sickness; acceptance is a blessing.

Consideration/Discussion

1.   Friendship: Discuss what friendship means to you. What are your

expectations of a friend? What expectations do you have of yourself in being a friend to others? Friendship is hard work entailing love, loyalty, and risk of disappointment.

2. Have you ever had to depend on a friend for a major matter? Did your friend come through for you?

3. Discuss what one of the following friendship sayings means to you.

Friendship Sayings

A friend is one who walks in when the world walks out. *Unknown*

A true friend is the best possession. *Ben Franklin (1706-1790)*

Keep your friendships in repair. *Samuel Butler (1612-1680)*

Make a friend when you don't need one. *Jamaican saying*

Misfortune tests the sincerity of friends. *Aesop (c. 620-560 BCE)*

Strangers are friends waiting to happen. *Unknown*

You never really know your friends from your enemies until the ice breaks. *Eskimo saying*

One of the most beautiful qualities of true friendship is to understand and to be understood. *Lucius Annaeus Seneca*

There is nothing on earth more to be prized than true friendship. *Thomas Aquinas*

Walking with a friend in the dark is better than walking alone in the light. *Helen Keller*

Friends show their love in times of trouble, not in happiness. *Euripides*

Chapter 34. David's Reign
(2 Samuel 2-7, 11-12)

Introduction

The Second Book of Samuel describes David's reign as king. He had to fight separatists within Israel and unite the nation. While he was completely devoted to God and able to win the loyalty of the Israelites, he also committed terrible, selfish sins. Yet his achievements so impressed the Israelites that during their time in exile they yearned for a king like David, a son of David, a descendant who would be like him.

During David's reign Israel continued its transition from small villages and twelve tribes dependent on farming and herding to a nation with growing cities and increasing economic, political, and military power.

Israel & Judah

After learning of Saul's death, David asked God if he should take control of the tribe of Judah in the southern part of Israel with its capital in Hebron. God agreed. David respectfully did so and met with the people. They publicly anointed David as their king. However, Abner, the commander of Saul's army, took control of Israel's other tribes in the north and made Ishbosheth, Saul's son, the king of Israel. The rivalry and fighting between Israel and Judah continued for years. Unbeknownst to David, Abner and then Ishbosheth were murdered. David, who had earlier declared his loyalty to Saul and promised to care for his descendants was profoundly saddened. All the tribes then proclaimed their loyalty to David; Israel and Judah were united as Israel again. They publicly anointed David at the age of 30 as their king of Judah and Israel combined.

Jerusalem

Jerusalem was a key, hilltop city occupied by the Jebusites. It was located at the crossroads of two trading routes and securely fortified by walls. As David and his army gathered below the city to attack, the Jebusites mocked them saying, "You will never get in here; even the blind and the crippled could keep you out." (2 Samuel 5:6) (GNT) David and his men overcame them with his strategy of sneaking through the water tunnel serving Jerusalem and then mounting a surprise attack from within the city. Subsequently, David made Jerusalem the capital of Israel. It had the advantage of not being previously occupied by any of the twelve tribes of Israel. Therefore, no tribe was being favored as the site of the new capital. In addition, Jerusalem was centrally located within Israel and at the crossroads of two major trading routes which made it an ideal place for governing and conducting business.

Before long the Philistines attacked Israel. David consulted God who provided him with a successful battle strategy that also enabled the Israelites to re-capture the Covenant Box which the Philistines had captured in a battle years before. The Covenant Box was considered a symbol of their nation's God. The Philistines' capture of the Covenant Box was an insult to the pride of the Israelites and a symbol of the Philistines' supremacy over them.

After their victory David and his army of 30,000 men marched behind the Covenant Box to Jerusalem. Crowds were singing and shouting joyously, trumpets were blaring, and David was dancing in the street. Michal, David's wife, saw him from her window and was disgusted with him.

Later she took him to task for acting like a fool. David strongly disagreed and said that he was dancing to honor God. Michal and David separated and never had any children.

Davidic Covenant

David realized that God had not only made him king but made his kingdom prosperous. Yet, he became upset that he was living in a beautiful cedar house while the Covenant Box of God was housed in a tent. David decided to build a temple for the Covenant Box. However, the prophet, Nathan, visited him with a message from God. David was not to build a temple for God. His son will build it. God had traveled with the Israelites in a tent all these years. God had been with them all this time and made David, their ruler. God said, "You will always have descendants, and I will make your kingdom last forever. Your dynasty will never end." (2 Samuel 7:16) (GNT) This is known as the Davidic Covenant, a covenant promising that David's descendants will live on forever. Many believe that the Davidic Covenant lives on through Jesus, a descendant of David, and the Christian Church founded on his teachings.

David and Bathsheba

David continued to be successful in military victories, including defeats of the Philistines, the Moabites, the Syrians, and the Ammonites. One afternoon while walking in his palace's rooftop garden, he saw a beautiful woman taking a bath in her house across the way. He learned that she was Bathsheba, the wife of Uriah, an officer in his army who was then attacking the Ammonite city of Rabbah. David had Bathsheba brought to him. They made love. She became pregnant while her husband was still on the front. David tried to cover up his adultery by having Uriah brought home on leave to spend a few nights with his wife. The plan failed because Uriah did not believe it was right for him to be home with his wife while his fellow officers and his troops were camping in the open near the battlefield. So, he slept at the palace gate with the king's guards. Next, David wrote a letter to Uriah's commander ordering him to put Uriah on the front line in the center where the fighting would be the heaviest, where Uriah would most likely be killed. And he was. When Bethsheba learned of her husband's death, she mourned. After the period of mourning, David had her brought to the palace. He married her, and they had a son. However, God was not pleased with David.

Nathan's Message

God sent his prophet Nathan to see David. Nathan told him a parable (a short story with a moral lesson) of a rich man and a poor man. While the rich man had many cattle and sheep, the poor man had only one lamb which had grown up with his children. The lamb was like a member of the family. One day a visitor came to the rich man's house. The rich man needed to provide hospitality but did not want to kill one of his own animals to prepare a meal for the visitor. Instead he took the poor man's lamb.

David was angry about the rich man and said he should die and pay four times as much as he took. Nathan, in turn, told David that he was that man when he took Uriah's wife. David immediately repented and said he had sinned against God. Nathan informed him that God forgave him, that he would not die, but, because of his misdeed, his child would die. And so, a week after his birth David's son died. Nathan had also predicted that someone from each subsequent generation would die a violent death and that someone from his family would cause trouble for him.

Solomon

David and Bathsheba mourned and comforted each other. Eventually they had another son, Solomon.

Israel under David

The beginnings of a modern state formed under David: a single ruler, a standing army, a national religion, the organization of a government (e.g., the collection of taxes, the appointment of local officials subject to David, etc.). Under David religion moved from a tribal focus to a national one with the installation of the ark in Jerusalem. He also unified the country with the selection of Jerusalem as its capital. The poor country became wealthy with David's conquests and the resulting additions to the national treasury. However, there were still some problems. The local tribes were not used to central authority and resisted at times. They relished their local authority. There was some sectional rivalry between the north and the south with sporadic revolts. There was a need for a comprehensive judicial system. He was a brilliant military and political leader and a faithful follower of God's commands. He did commit serious sins, but he readily acknowledged them and accepted his punishment. Overall, David was without an equal in Israel's history.

Notes

1. Jerusalem is a sacred city to three of the world's major religions. The Jews revere the remains of the wall from the Great temple built by King Herod and destroyed by the Romans in 70 CE. For Christians this is the city where Jesus was crucified. For Muslims Jerusalem contains the Dome of the Rock, a mosque built over the site where all three religions believe Abraham took his son to be sacrificed. More than half of the world's religious believers belong to these three religions.

2. The Book of Psalms is a book of sacred Israelite songs and poems traditionally attributed to David. While there is some dispute about his authorship of the entire collection, 73 of the 150 psalms were marked "of David."

3. Hebron was an important, ancient Israelite city about 20 miles south

of Jerusalem and a gathering place for the southern tribes of Israel. Hebron was where the men of Judah anointed David as their king. It served as David's capital for about seven years before Judah and Israel combined.

4.   Religion. Early sites where Israelites worshiped and held religious feasts were at Shiloh, Bethel, Gilgal, Mizpah, and Beersheba.

Commentary

1.   Israel's Prosperity under David. The poor nation of Israel under Saul became wealthier under David with his conquests. For example, the conquered Ammonites were enslaved to make bricks. In the north his conquests brought copper ore and other metals to Israel. His conquests brought jewels, gold, and other loot.

2.   Temple. Until now there had been no interest in building a permanent home for the Ark of the Covenant. You might view it as a bit of anti-temple tradition in the Old Testament. A special tent (the Tabernacle) housed the Ark of the Covenant and symbolized where God could periodically visit the people. (Recall the symbolism of the ziggurat in Mesopotamia as a place for their gods to visit their people on earth.) When the Israelites moved, so did the tent. God was always with them. However, a permanent temple would put God in one place. It would localize God and diminish his presence among the tribes. The notion of a stagnant location of a temple flew in face of the earlier notion of a movable, dynamic God.

3.   Reasons to Delay the Construction of the Temple. On a practical level David was busy trying to consolidate the twelve tribes into an effective, unified nation. He needed to build a government, organize an army, construct forts, and settle the issues of the twelve tribes and conquered lands for the first time as a nation of Israel. There was a lot of first-time work to do without precedent to guide him.

Chapter 35. David's Sons (2 Samuel 13-19) An Out of Control Son!

David Is Not a Perfect Hero

The man who had been a fugitive from King Saul, the man who had wandered from cave to cave hiding from King Saul and his army, was now the king of Israel. Thousands of people worked in his fields and shops. They built his palace, forts, and storerooms for crops. David had reached his ultimate glory.

However, like a true Israelite hero, the roller coaster ride was about to begin. While David was a success as a warrior and as a king, he was a sad failure as a father to his large family of many wives and children.

David's son, Absalom, was the king's favorite son. Absalom's charm made him popular with everyone. He was anxious to be the king. However, he was the second oldest son. Absalom became jealous of his older brother, Amnon. The jealousy turned to hatred and finally a plot to succeed his father, David, as the king.

A Murder in the Family: Exile—Who Will Be the Next King?

While Absalom did not kill Amnon, he did order his slaves to do it. The royal household was so enraged that Absalom had to flee for his life and remain in exile. Although David missed his favorite son, he knew he must keep Absalom in exile both as a punishment and for protection.

Absalom wanted to return, and he still wanted to become the king.

Joab, David's army commander, and others kept asking David to allow Absalom to return. After three years in exile, David finally agreed to let Absalom return on the condition that Absalom live quietly in his own house. David even refused to see his son.

For two years David did not talk to Absalom. However, David was getting old. People began to talk about who would succeed David. Some thought another son, Adonijah, would become the king. Some thought the king should be selected by all the people. Others wanted David to name his successor.

Bathsheba who was David's favorite wife had a son named Solomon. She wanted her son to be the next king. There was a rumor that David had promised her that her son would succeed him. Maybe this was why David refused to speak to Absalom.

Absalom who was still popular began to spend more time with the common people. He often stood by the city gate and offered advice and occasionally settled disputes. The people loved him. He would wonder aloud that, if he was a judge, then every man could plead his case with him.

A Son's Revolt against His Father

Finally, Absalom planned a revolt against his father. Absalom and a large number of friends went to Hebron. As Absalom arrived in the ancient city, his friends lined the streets, blew trumpets, and shouted, "Absalom is king in Hebron." Because of dissatisfaction elsewhere with David's policies as king (e.g., taxes, conscription, centralized authority, etc.), Absalom's friends were able to spread the revolt. Only the people in Jerusalem did not join the revolt, perhaps because David's large army was there.

When the news of the revolt reached Jerusalem, the broken-hearted king decided to flee at once. He was not prepared to fight. David and his family and servants left the city of which he had been so proud. Meanwhile, Absalom occupied the city without a fight.

David and his commander, Joab, regrouped and prepared for battle.

David, still the ever-loving father of a traitorous son, told his commander to deal gently with Absalom. Joab's hastily gathered troops started out. Before the rebels could take their position, Joab attacked. Taken by surprise, Absalom's raw recruits became afraid and retreated in a confused state. Absalom, who feared that he might be captured, tried to hide in the nearby woods. While riding his donkey, Absalom failed to dodge some low-hanging branches. His head was caught in the fork of a branch lifting him from his donkey, stunned and dying, while his donkey galloped on.

A Death in the Family

Joab came upon Absalom and, without a moment's thought, he thrust his spear into Absalom three times killing him.

A runner carried the news of Joab's victory and Absalom's death to David. The king was stricken with grief. He stayed in his room for days. The people of Jerusalem were preparing to celebrate the victory but stopped when they learned of David's grief. When Joab and his victorious army arrived in Jerusalem, Joab had to convince David to at least come out and thank his troops.

David finally did thank the troops. He issued a pardon to everyone who participated in the rebellion. All was peaceful again in Jerusalem with the aging David back in his palace. But everyone knew that the frail king would not live much longer. They still asked, "Who will become king after David?"

Commentary

1.   Like many of their heroes, the Israelites describe David with all his great attributes and his flaws and weaknesses. He is just like many of us, not perfect.

2.   This chapter in David's life reminds us of the challenge many of us face in our families – a challenge to deal with severe adversity in the loving manner as a devoted family member. Sometimes it sends us to the depths of our souls for strength and perseverance we did not know we had.

Consideration/Discussion

Think of the time you or another family member had to help a family member with an extremely difficult matter. How did you find the strength to do it? To overcome your natural reluctance?

Chapter 36. Solomon (1 Kings 1-11)

Adonijah Tries to Succeed David

With Absalom dead and David dying in old age, Adonijah decided he should be the king. He was handsome and the oldest surviving son. He had done everything expected of him. So, he gathered his horses, chariots, and an escort of fifty men. He obtained the support of Joab, a general in David's army, and of Abiathar, a priest. Along with many king's officials and the other sons of King David, they gathered at Snake Rock for a sacrificial feast of sheep, bulls, and cattle. However, he did not invite Solomon or Nathan or the king's bodyguards.

When Nathan learned of Adonijah's gathering to make him the king, he alerted Bathsheba who approached David. "Your Majesty, you made a solemn promise in the name of God that my Solomon would succeed you as king. But Adonijah has already become king, and you don't know anything about it." (1 Kings 1:17-18) (GNT) David announced he would fulfill that promise today. He had his court officials escort Solomon on David's donkey to Gihon Springs where he instructed Nathan to publicly anoint Solomon as the next king in front of the gathered people. With trumpets blaring and people shouting, "Long live King Solomon," he was anointed as the next king.

As the news reached Adonijah's guests, they became afraid and left him. Adonijah, too, feared David's reaction and sent a message to David pledging his loyalty and begging not to be killed. David agreed and sent his son, Adonijah, home.

Solomon's Wise Judgment

After ruling Israel for forty years David died, and Solomon succeeded him. He made an alliance with Egypt and married the king of Egypt's daughter. Solomon offered sacrifices to God. In a dream he tells God that he is young and inexperienced. He asks for the wisdom to rule his people justly and to know the difference between good and evil. God was impressed that he did not ask for self-centered things, such as riches, a long life, or battle victories. He promised Solomon wisdom and also wealth and honor if he keeps God's laws as David did. Despite David's very serious flaws (i.e., stealing another man's wife, arranging so that man gets killed in battle, and being a poor father with out of control sons), David faithfully obeyed all of God's laws and commands. When Solomon awoke, he realized he had spoken to God. He made an offering to God in thanks.

Two women, one holding a new born baby and the other without a child, came before King Solomon to decide a childhood custody dispute. The childless woman claimed that both gave birth a couple of days apart, but the other woman's baby died. The childless woman claimed that the other mother accidentally rolled over in her sleep and smothered her baby. While the childless mother was sleeping, the woman whose baby died switched the dead baby for the live baby. When she awoke, she immediately recognized that the dead baby was not hers. They had both been staying in the same house, and no one else was present. They argued back and forth in front of the king. "The living baby is mine." "No, it's mine…" The king asked for his sword and instructed his staff to cut the living baby in two. Give each woman a half. The real mother with her heart full of love and sorrow screamed, "Don't cut the child. Give it to the other woman." The other woman said, "Neither of us should have it. Go ahead and cut the baby in two." Solomon instructed his staff to give the baby to the first woman for she was the real mother whose first desire was to save the child's life. When the people of Israel heard of the decision, they were filled with respect for their new king and his ability to settle cases so fairly.

Solomon's Prosperity

Under his reign Solomon and the Israelites prospered. The Israelites continued to grow in numbers. Each family had its own grapevines and fig trees. Solomon divided Israel into twelve districts with an appointed governor. Each district was responsible for furnishing the king and his palace with all their needs one month each year. Each day he needed 150 bushels of flour, 300 bushels of meal, 10 stall-fed cattle, 20 pasture-fed cattle, and 100 sheep plus deer, poultry, barley, and straw. He had 12,000 cavalry horses and 40,000 chariot horses. Solomon expanded the kingdom to include all the nations from the Euphrates River to the Egyptian border. Those nations paid a tribute (tax) to him, but everyone lived in peace.

Solomon's Wisdom

Solomon was considered to be a man of unusual wisdom and insight, wiser than any of the wise men of that era. He wrote numerous proverbs and songs, perhaps as many as 3,000 proverbs and 1,000 songs, although some scholars believe these numbers were symbolic of a lot of writing and not the actual number written. He was also knowledgeable about the plant and animal world. Kings from all over sent staff to consult with Solomon.

Solomon Builds a Temple and a Palace

Solomon realized that his father, David, was constantly fighting wars to establish the kingdom of Israel in Canaan which was occupied by other people. Although his father could not build a temple for worship to God in such circumstances, Solomon was blessed with peace on his borders and with no enemies. Solomon was known for his diplomacy skills as he had productive relations with all the nearby nations. King Hiram of Tyre, a Phoenician king just to the north of Israel in Lebanon, had been a friend of David and became a strong supporter of Solomon. So, Solomon asked King Hiram for his help in building a temple. He requested King Hiram's men to cut down cedars in Lebanon, float them down the coast to Israel, and help construct a temple with the aid of Israelites. He offered to pay the King's men whatever the king decided. King Hiram was pleased with the request and agreed. Solomon provided Israelites to help and provided 100,000 bushels of wheat and 110,000 gallons of olive oil annually to feed King Hiram's men.

King Solomon forced 30,000 Israelite men to work one month every three months in Lebanon, 10,000 men at a time. In Israel he also had 80,000 stone cutters, 70,000 laborers and 3,300 foremen working on the project. In the fourth year of Solomon's reign construction began on the temple. It was finished seven years later. Then he built a huge palace for himself, a project that took thirteen years to complete.

Some of the forced laborers were descendants of the people the Israelites had conquered. While the Israelites were not enslaved, they did serve as Solomon's soldiers, officers, foremen, and court officials.

Queen Sheba's Visit

The queen of Sheba heard of Solomon's fame and decided to visit him. She brought a large group of attendants and probably traveled by camel to Jerusalem from Ethiopia. She brought gifts of spices, jewels, and gold. When they met, she asked him all kinds of questions. None was too difficult for him to answer. She was impressed with his wisdom, his wealth, his beautiful palace, his well-organized staff, and the sacrifices he offered in the temple. He presented her with impressive gifts. The queen of Sheba and her attendants returned home after their visit.

Solomon's Temptations

Even though God had commanded the Israelites not to marry polytheistic believing women (out of fear the Israelites would lose their faith in their one God), Solomon loved and married several foreign women. Eventually they led him away from his one God. By the time of his old age, he not only actively worshipped foreign gods, but he had also built places of worship to foreign gods. Despite David's many faults, he was always faithful to God. Despite Solomon's unbelievable wealth and successes in life due to God, he was not faithful. Because of his unfaithfulness, God told Solomon that he would take the kingdom away from his son and give it to one of his officials. Out of respect for his father, David, God left one tribe with Solomon's son.

The Revolt: Israel Splits

And so, it came to be that after Solomon's death in 931 BCE, the northern tribes revolted. The people had resented the hardships they experienced under Solomon's forty years of rule: the forced labor and heavy taxes. Jeroboam became the king of the northern tribes called Israel with its capital at Shechem. He ruled for twenty-two years. Solomon's son, Rehoboam, became the king of Judah and ruled the nation called Judah for seventeen years from Jerusalem. The golden age of a unified Israel ended with Solomon's death. Later the Assyrians conquered Israel in 721 BCE; the Babylonians conquered Judah in 586 BCE.

Notes

1.   The time from the Judges to King Solomon was a transition period from small villages dependent on farming and herding to the growth of cities with economic, political and military power.

2.   Solomon's temple followed the three-room Canaanite model: an outer chamber for the people, a middle chamber for the priests and nobles,

and a sanctuary called the Holy of Holies that only the high priest could go into once a year. Solomon's temple was 90 feet long, 30 feet wide, and 45 feet high. Ivory covered the outer doors; gold decorated the walls of the holiest room; cedar beams from Lebanon formed the roof. People could offer sacrifices on the stone altar in the temple's courtyard. Nearby was a bronze basin that the priests could use to wash before entering the temple. Nothing of Solomon's temple, palace, and administrative complex survives.

3.   Modern scholars believe the Queen of Sheba was from the Kingdom of Axum in Ethiopia or the Kingdom of Yemen or both. They are only 15 miles (25km) apart by water. She traveled by camel to Jerusalem and brought frankincense, myrrh, gold, and precious jewels. Frankincense is made from the sap of desert trees that only grow in these two areas. She became a follower of Yahweh. Some believe this is how Judaism came to Ethiopia. She spent time with Solomon, became pregnant in Israel, and gave birth to a son, Menelik, in Ethiopia. According to Ethiopian legend he returned to see his father and came home with an Ark of the Covenant. Menelik is the first in an unbroken line of Ethiopian kings into the 20th century.

4.   Solomon's marriages to foreign women may have been made for political and military purposes. The formation of such resulting alliances had been used by monarchs through the centuries.

5.   Solomon's Accomplishments. Solomon is remembered for his legendary wisdom and for building the temple that became the focus of the Israelite religion. He fortified and expanded the wall around Jerusalem, fortified Megiddo, Gezer, and Hazor as bases for his chariot divisions, built a huge palace, and built a fleet on the Red Sea for trade with Arabia and East Africa. He taxed caravans to help pay for these accomplishments.

Consideration/Discussion

1. Discuss how the following samples of Solomon's proverbs relate to your life today.

Proverbs Chapter 10:

> 10:9. Honest people are safe and secure, but the dishonest will be caught.
>
> 10:20. A good person's words are like pure silver; a wicked person's ideas are worthless.
>
> 13:18. Someone who will not learn will be poor and disgraced. Anyone who listens to correction is respected.
>
> 18:2. A fool does not care whether he understands a thing or not; all he wants to do is to show how smart he is.
>
> 25:21. If your enemies are hungry, feed them; if they are thirsty, give them a drink.

2. The reigns of David and Solomon are considered to be the Golden Age of Israel when it was prosperous and respected among nations. Notice how David started as a poor shepherd and became a successful warrior and leader of the Israelites despite his repeated, serious sins of character. Solomon was wealthy and wise beyond his contemporaries but not faithful to his one God. Discuss the positive and negative lessons learned from each in terms of friendship, humility, respect shown, taking responsibility, leadership, and religious values.

3. Falling away from one's commitments and religious beliefs can have consequences. As the Israelites were suffering through the oppression of their exile to Babylonia, they reflected on their past disloyalty to their faith to explain their situation. Their reflection offered a path forward, that is, through a renewed commitment to their faith. Consider how a renewed commitment to your core principles can improve your life.

Chapter 37. Esther (Esther 1-9)

Exile

King Xerxes ruled Persia (which included ancient Babylon, Assyria, Israel, and Egypt) from his capital in the city of Susa from 486-464 BCE. At that time Persia had 127 provinces from India to Ethiopia. In Susa a Jewish man named Mordecai was among the Jews exiled to Persia when King Nebuchadnezzar of Babylon conquered Judah. He adopted his orphaned cousin, Esther, whose name in Persian means "the maiden was beautiful and lovely." He raised her as his own daughter. They both worked in the king's court. He advised Esther not to reveal their Jewish background.

A New Queen

As luck would have it, the king noticed Esther and took a liking to her. He decided to make her the queen in place of his estranged wife, Vashti, who four years earlier had greatly upset the king with her refusal to attend one of his banquets. He held a banquet in Esther's honor, placed the royal crown on her head, and made her the queen in place of Vashti. He proclaimed a holiday in celebration.

A Death Threat

While Mordecai was working in an administrative position in the king's court, he learned that two of the king's staff members planned to assassinate the king. Mordecai told Queen Esther who informed the king. An investigation confirmed Mordecai's report. The two men were executed. Mordecai's service was recorded in the court records.

Haman's Plot

Soon afterward the king promoted a man named Haman to his prime minister position. The king ordered all his officials to bow and kneel before Haman to show their respect. As a Jew Mordecai refused to bow and kneel. Haman was furious. He decided to not only punish Mordecai but to kill every Jew in all of Persia. Haman ordered lots (numbered stones called purim and similar to dice today) to be cast to find the right day and month to carry out his plot. The date cast was the thirteenth day of the twelfth month of Adar.

Haman told the king, "There is a certain race of people scattered all over your empire and found in every province. They observe customs that are not like those of any other people. Moreover, they do not obey the laws of the empire, so it is not in your best interest to tolerate them. If it please your majesty, issue a decree that they are to be put to death. If you do, I guarantee that I will be able to put 375 tons of silver into the royal treasury for the administration of the empire." (Esther 3:8-9) (GNT) The king agreed but declined the money. He gave Haman his ring to stamp the needed proclamations.

Haman had the proclamations drawn up in all the languages needed and then distributed throughout the empire in time for the chosen date, the thirteenth day of the twelfth month of Adar. All the Jews were to be executed on that day and their possessions confiscated. Throughout the empire there was a huge uproar among the Jews. They fasted, prayed, wailed (a mournful cry), and wore their mourning clothes. Mordecai, too, was in his mourning clothes. When her servants told her what he was wearing, Esther sent for Mordecai to find out what was going on. Mordecai gave her a copy of Haman's proclamation and asked her to plead with the king to have mercy on her people.

Esther's Plan

At first Esther was frustrated. People, including the queen, can see the king only if summoned before him. According to the law, if someone sees the king without being summoned, that person must die. Mordecai told her, "Don't imagine that you are safer than any other Jew because you are in the royal palace." (Esther 4:13) (GNT) She told Mordecai that she would go to the king even if she must die for doing so.

Esther put on her royal robes and stood at the outer edge of the inner courtyard facing the king inside. When he saw Queen Esther, he motioned with his gold scepter for her to come in. When he asked what she wanted, she replied that she would like him and Haman to be her guests at a banquet she was preparing for them that night. At her banquet she invited them to come the next evening as her guests at another banquet. Then she would tell the king what she wanted.

Haman's Plan

Haman left the first banquet in good spirits at the honor given to him to dine with the king and queen. However, as he left the palace, he saw Mordecai who did not rise or bow or show him any sign of respect. Haman was furious. His friends and his wife listened to him ranting how his long list of successes meant nothing as long as Mordecai did not respect him by bowing. They suggested that he have a gallows built 75 feet high and ask the king tomorrow morning to have Mordecai hanged on it. That way he could go to the second banquet happy.

A Restless Night

It just so happened on the same evening Haman plotted to have Mordecai hanged, the king was unable to sleep. So, he had the court records read to him to put him to sleep. However, when the servant read the account of how Mordecai reported the plot to assassinate the king, King Xerxes asked how Mordecai had been honored. Upon learning that nothing had been done, the king asked if any officials were in the palace. Haman who had just arrived to ask the king's permission to hang Mordecai was ushered in. The king said to him, "There is someone I wish very much to honor. What should I do for this man?"

Haman thought that the king wanted to honor him. He suggested that the man be dressed in royal robes, that a royal ornament be put on the king's horse, and that the king's highest nobleman lead the man mounted on the horse through the city square while announcing, "This is how the king rewards those he honors."

Mordecai Honored

The king agreed and told Haman to get the robes and horse for Mordecai the Jew. You will find him at the entrance to the palace. Haman did as instructed and led Mordecai dressed in royal robes and mounted on the king's horse with a royal ornament through the city square while announcing, "This is how the king rewards those he honors." When they finished, Mordecai returned to the palace entrance; Haman went home in embarrassment. His wife and friends told him that he was losing power to Mordecai.

A Decision

Haman went with the king to Esther's second banquet that evening. Over wine the king asked her again what she wanted. He promised she would have it. She asked that she and her people may live for they had been sold for slaughter. When the king asked who would dare do such a thing, Esther said this man, Haman. The king left in a fury for the palace gardens. Haman who was now in fear for his life begged the queen for mercy. When the king returned to the room and learned that Haman had just built a gallows for Mordecai, the king ordered Haman to be hanged. And he was hanged on the gallows he built for Mordecai. The king gave his ring with its seal to Mordecai and made him a key official in his palace.

One More Request

Esther told the king that she was related to Mordecai. She made one more request. She begged the king to overrule the proclamation that Haman had issued in his name to slaughter the Jews throughout the empire on the thirteenth day of the twelfth month of Adar. The king noted that he could not revoke a proclamation issued in his name and stamped with the royal seal. However, she or Mordecai could write the Jews whatever she wanted in his name and stamp it with the royal seal.

A Plan to Save the Jews

Mordecai dictated a decree to the governors, administrators, and officials in all of the 127 provinces in the empire. The letter permitted the Jews to organize for their own self-defense. If they were attacked, they could fight back, kill their attackers, and take their possessions. The decree was delivered throughout the land by riders on royal horses. Jews filled the streets everywhere in relief and joy.

On the day chosen for their destruction the Jews attacked their enemies and destroyed them over that day and the next one. In fact, the governors, administrators, and officials helped the Jews because they knew Mordecai was now a powerful official in the king's court.

Mordecai and Esther sent letters to all the Persian Jews telling them to observe two days as holidays to celebrate their deliverance from Haman's planned slaughter. The Jews followed the instruction. The celebration became an annual custom, known as the Festival of Purim. (Remember the lots called "purim" that Haman threw to select the date for slaughtering the Jews.)

Notes

1. The Purim holiday is often celebrated in the late winter or early spring by reading the Book of Esther and sharing food and gifts with

family and the less fortunate. Adults may prepare by fasting for a day; children may wear costumes.

2.   Lots were numbered stones used in ancient times to determine favorable conditions or request divine guidance. Gambling today with dice or playing the lottery (derived from the root word lot) are modern day customs using random numbers.

Commentary

1.   The Book of Esther reads like a short novel full of twists and turns. The author is unknown and may have been a Persian Jew living in exile at the time of King Xerxes's reign. The author provides a vivid account of the court and the empire at that time.

2.   Interestingly the book does not contain the word God or any prayers in the Hebrew version. Both were later added to the Greek translation. There was some reluctance by the Jewish and Catholic leaders to include the Book of Esther among the books selected for their official holy scriptures since there is no mention of God or prayers. It may have been included to explain the Purim holiday observed by Jews. The Purim is not mentioned in any other book. The Persian Jews brought the holiday with them to Jerusalem when they returned from their exile.

3.   The Book of Esther has two themes: Hatred brings destruction. People in high places have a responsibility to help those who are powerless.

Consideration/Discussion

1.   What issues are you facing or have faced that required courage? What risks did you take?

2. How tolerant are you of people who are different from you (e.g., race, nationality, class, income, residence, interests in sports, politics, religion, and other pastimes)? How tolerant should we be? Why?

3. Discuss the significance of Mordecai's quote for all of us: "Don't imagine that you are safer than any other Jew because you are in the royal palace." (Esther 4:13)

APPENDIX

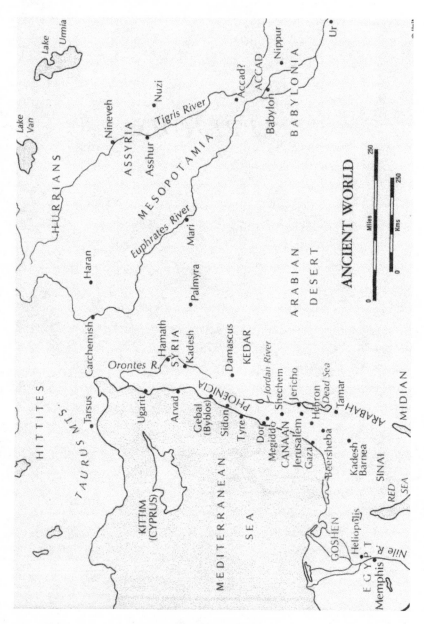

Ancient World Map

Good News Bible Today's English Version — Second Edition ©1992, p. 1533.
Maps © United Bible Societies, 1976, 1978. All rights reserved.

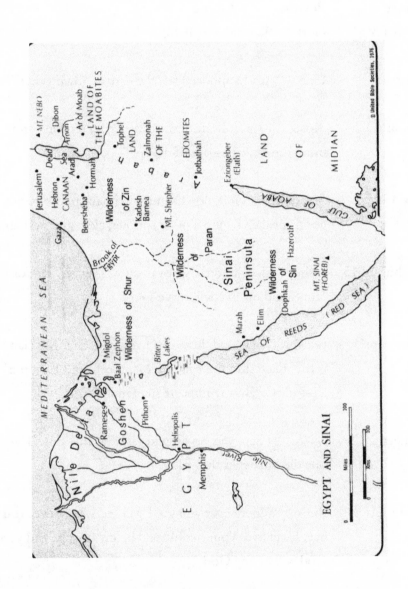

Egypt & Sinai Map

Good News Bible Today's English Version – Second Edition ©*1992, p. 1534. Maps* © *United Bible Societies, 1976, 1978. All rights reserved.*

Famous Quotes

Place	Person	Quote
Gen 1:3	God	"Let there be light."
Gen 4:9	Cain	"Am I supposed to take care of my brother?"
Ex 3:113.	Moses	"I am nobody. How can I go to the king and bring the Israelites out of Egypt?"
Ex 4:104.	Moses	"No, God, don't send me. I have never been a good speaker...I am a poor speaker, slow and hesitant."
Joshua 24:15	Joshua	"Decide today whom you will serve...As for my family and me, we will serve God."
Judges 6:15	Gideon	"But God, how can I rescue Israel? My clan is the weakest in the tribe of Manasseh, and I am the least important member of my family."
Judges 21:25	---	"There was no king in Israel at that time. Every one did whatever they pleased."
Ruth 1:16	Ruth	"Where ever you go, I will go. Where ever you live, I will live. Your people will be my people, and your God will be my God."
1 Samuel 9:21	Saul:	"I belong to the tribe of Benjamin, the smallest tribe of Israel, and my family is the least important one in the tribe. Why, then do you talk to me like this?"

1 Samuel 16:7 God   But God said to him, "Pay no attention to how tall and handsome he is. I have rejected him, because I do not judge as people judge. They look at the outward appearance, but I look at the heart."

1 Samuel 24:17 Saul   "You are right, and I am wrong. You have been so good to me, while I have done such wrong to you!... How often does someone catch an enemy and then let him go away unharmed?"

1 Kings 3:9   Solomon "Give me the wisdom I need to rule your people with justice and to know the difference between good and evil."

Esther 4:13   Mordecai: "Don't imagine that you are safer than any other Jew because you are in the royal palace."

Bibliography

Good News Bible, New York: American Bible Society, 1992.

Armento, Beverly J. et al, *A Message of Ancient Days*, Boston: Houghton Mifflin, 2003.

Boadt, Lawrence, *Reading the Old Testament, An Introduction*, New York: Paulist Press, 1984.

Break Through! The Bible for Young Catholics. Winona, MN: Saint Mary's Press, 2006.

Buehrens, John. *Understanding the Bible*. Boston: Beacon Press, 2003.

Burstein, Stanley M. and Shek, Richard, *Ancient Civilizations through the Renaissance*. Boston: Houghton Mifflin Harcourt, 2012

The Catholic Youth Bible. Winona, WI: Saint Mary's Press, 2000.

Comay, Joan. *Who's Who in the Bible.* New York: Wings Books, 1971.

Feiler, Bruce. *Walking the Bible.* New York: William Marrow, 2001.

Geoghegan, Jeffrey & Homan, Michael. *The Bible for Dummies,* Hoboken, N.J.: Joh Wiley & Sons, 2003

Genesis to Revelation, Volume 1: Genesis to Esther, Teacher Book. Nashville: Abington Press, 1997.

Gibbs Binkley, Cheryl and McKeel, Jane M., *Living the Promise,* Self-published with the Unitarian Church of Arlington, VA. Date unknown.

Good News Bible, Today's English Version. New York: American Bible Society, 1992.

Halley's Bible Handbook, Grand Rapids, MI: Zondervan, 2000.

Haney Schafer, Mary. *The Bible & Its Influence*—Teacher's Edition. New York: BLP Publishing, 2006.

Isbouts, Jean-Pierre. *The Biblical World: An Illustrated Atlas,* Washington, DC: National Geographic Society, 2007.

Kagan, Neil, *Concise History of the World,* Washington, DC: National Geographic Society, 2006.

Keller-Scholz, Rick & Pomanowski, Jeannie. *Break Through! The Bible for Young Catholics, Teacher's Activity Manual.* Winona, MN: St. Mary's Press, 2006.

Nichols, John. *A Wind Swept over Waters: Reflections on 60 Favorite Bible Passages.* Boston: Skinner House Books, 2007.

Pineo, Caroline, *Cain's Children, A Course of Study.* Philadelphia: Friends General Conference, 1970.

Reed Newland, Mary, *Teaching Manual for Written on Our Hearts: The Old Testament Story of God's Love,* Winona, MN: Saint Mary's Press, 2002

Sanders, Nancy I. *Old Testament Days An Activity Guide*. Chicago: Chicago Review Press, 1999.

Student Activity Workbook for Break Through. Winona, MN: St. Marty's Press, 2006.

Walker, Catherine B. *Bible Workbook*, Volume 1, Old Testament, Chicago: Moody Press, 1952

Williams, Derek. *The Biblical Times*. Grand Rapids, MI: Baker Books, 1997.

Website Resources

"What Does It Mean to Be Human." *Humanorigins.si.edu*. Smithsonian National Museum of Natural History, 26 September 2019. Web. 06 October 2019.
http://humanorigins.si.edu/evidence/human-fossils/species/homo-sapiens

Riess, Jana. "Religious Nones Are Gaining Ground in America and They're Worried about the Economy." *Religionnews.com*. Religion News Service, 16 November 2017. Web. 06 October 2019.
https://religionnews.com/2017/11/16/religious-nones-are-gaining-ground-in-america-and-theyre-worried-about-the-economy-says-new-study/

Emba, Christine. "Even Atheists Should Read the Bible." (online title). "You Should Read the Bible." (print title). *Washingtonpost.com*. Washington Post, 30 March 2018. Web. 06 October 2019.
https://www.washingtonpost.com/opinions/even-atheists-should-read-the-bible/2018/03/30/98a1133c-3444-11e8-94fa-32d48460b955_story.html

"History of Circumcision." *Wikipedia.org*. Wikipedia, 01 October 2019. Web. 06 October 2019.
https://en.wikipedia.org/wiki/History_of_male_circumcision

Dias, Elizabeth. "The Mystery of the Bible's Phantom Camels." *Time.com*. Time USA, 11 February 2014. Web. 06 October 2019.
http://time.com/6662/the-mystery-of-the-bibles-phantom-camels/

Zonszein, Mairav. "Domesticated Camels Come to Israel in 930, B.C., Centuries Later than the Bible Says." *Nationalgeographic.com*, National Geographic Society, 10 February 2014. Web. 06 October 2019.

https://news.nationalgeographic.com/news/2014/02/140210-domesticated-camels-israel-bible-archaeology-science/

"Joseph and the Amazing Technicolor Dreamcoat." *Wikipedia.org.* Wikipedia, 05 October 2019. Web. 06 October 2019.
https://en.wikipedia.org/wiki/Joseph_and_the_Amazing_Technicolor_Dreamcoat

"Egyptian Dream Scrying." *Crystalinks.com.* Crystalinks, Web. 06 October 2019.
http://www.crystalinks.com/egyptdreamscrying.html

"The Egyptian Dream Book." *Ancient-origins.net.* Ancient Origins, 04 May 2014. Web. 06 October 2019.
http://www.ancient-origins.net/myths-legends/egyptian-dream-book-001621

Crisp, Tom. "Egyptian (ancient) Dream Beliefs." *Dreamhawk.com.* Dreamhawk, Web. 06 October 2019.
http://dreamhawk.com/dream-encyclopedia/egyptian-dream-beliefs/

Wood, Michael. "The Queen of Sheba." *Pbs.org.* Educational Broadcasting Corporation. Web. 06 October 2019. http://www.pbs.org/mythsandheroes/myths_four_sheba.html

Chapter References

Bible Quotes: *Good News Bible,* New York: American Bible Society, 1992.

Chapter 1. Background: Who are we?
Concise History of the World, Kagan, Neil. Washington, D.C.: National Geographic Society, 2006, p. 16. Brain enlargement.

Armento, Beverly J. et al, *A Message of Ancient Days,* Boston: Houghton Mifflin, 2003, p. 91-95, 98-101, 106-113, 121-130, 158-159. Evolution of humans, farming, and polytheism.

Burstein, Stanley M. and Shek, Richard, *Ancient Civilizations through the Renaissance.* Boston: Houghton Mifflin Harcourt, 2012, p. 28-43, 62-63. Evolution of humans, farming, and polytheism.

http://humanorigins.si.edu/evidence/human-fossils/species/homo-sapiens
Evolution of humans.

https://www.nicepng.com/ourpic/u2e6w7u2w7u2e6a9_australopithecus-afa-rensis-australopithecus-afarensis-lucy-png/ Image of Australopithecus Afarensis Lucy.

Chapter 2. Introduction

Armento, Beverly J. et al, *A Message of Ancient Days*, Boston: Houghton Mifflin, 2003, p. 93, 158-159, 193. Neanderthal graves, Egyptian and Mesopotamian polytheism.

Burstein, Stanley M. and Shek, Richard, *Ancient Civilizations through the Renaissance*. Boston: Houghton Mifflin Harcourt, 2012, p. 40-43, 62-63. Agriculture and polytheism.

Boadt, Lawrence, *Reading the Old Testament, An Introduction*, New York: Paulist Press, 1984,. p. 11. Single most important source of Western culture, especially expressions and words.

Walker, Catherine B., *Bible Workbook*, Volume 1, Old Testament, Chicago: Moody Press, 1952, p. 4. Biblical influences in art and history.

Geoghegan, Jeffrey & Homan, Michael. *The Bible for Dummies*, Hoboken, N.J.: Joh Wiley & Sons, 2003, p. 1. Understanding the Bible.

Chapter 3. Geography: Civilizations, Topography & Seasons

Boadt, Lawrence, *Reading the Old Testament*. New York: Paulist Press, 1984, p. 31-36. Map and topography.

Halley's Bible Handbook, Grand Rapids, MI: Zondervan, 2000, p. 55-59. Topography and seasons.

Isbouts, Jean-Pierre. *The Biblical World, An Illustrated Atlas*. Washington, D.C.: National Geographic Society, 2007, p. 19. Topography.

Comay, Joan, *Who's Who in the Bible*. New York: Wings Books, 1971, p. 15. Topography.

Chapter 4. Weather & Roads in Biblical Times

Halley's Bible Handbook, Zondervan, 2000, p. 48-54, 80. Map. Roads and Routes in Canaan.

Chapter 5. Bible Organization

Halley's Bible Handbook, Grand Rapids, MI: Zondervan, 2000, p. 26. Bible books.

Gibbs Binkley, Cheryl and McKeel, Jane M. *Living the Promise*, Self-published with the Unitarian Church of Arlington, VA. Date unknown. p. 2-3, 8-10. Covenant and love.

Armento, Beverly J, et al. *A Message of Ancient Days*, Houghton Mifflin, 2003, p. 160-161. History of writing.

Chapter 6. Creation Introduction

Good News Bible, New York: American Bible Society, 1992, p. 1. Introduction to Genesis.

Chapter 7. Seven Days

Good News Bible, Today's English Version. New York: American Bible Society, 1992. Genesis 1-2. Creation of the world in seven days.

Chapter 8. Creation: Adam & Eve

Good News Bible, Today's English Version. New York: American Bible Society, 1992. Genesis 2-3. The Adam and Eve story.

Halley's Bible Handbook. Grand Rapids, Michigan: Zondervan, 2000, p. 92. Location of the Garden of Eden.

Comay, Joan, *Who's Who in the Bible*. New York: Wings Books, 1971, p. 38. The belief that Adam was created out of clay is similar to ancient Egyptian and Mesopotamian folk stories about creation.

Binkley, Cheryl Gibbs & McKeel, Jane M., *Living the Promise*. Self-published with the Unitarian Church of Arlington, VA. p. 17. Adam and Eve discussion questions.

Chapter 9. Cain & Abel

Good News Bible, Today's English Version. New York: American Bible Society, 1992, Genesis 4. Cain and Abel story.

Genesis to Revelation. Nashville: Abington Press, 1997, p. 17. General background information.

Gibbs Binkley, Cheryl & McKeel, Jane M., *Living the Promise.* Self-Published with the Unitarian Church of Arlington, VA, p. 20. Feelings of rejection.

Chapter 10. Noah & the Flood
Good News Bible, Today's English Version. New York: American Bible Society, 1992. Genesis 6-9. The Noah story.

Boadt, Lawrence, *Reading the Old Testament.* New York: Paulist Press, 1984, p. 114-116. Floodgates and land surrounded by water above and alongside the land.

Halley's Bible Handbook. Grand Rapids, MI: Zondervan, 2000, p. 97. Other flood traditions.

Chapter 11. Tower of Babel
Good News Bible, Today's English Version. New York: American Bible Society, 1992. Genesis 11. The Tower of Babel story.

Geoghegan, Jeffery & Homan, Michael, *The Bible for Dummies.* Hoboken, NJ: John A. Wiley & Sons, 2003, p. 66. Ziggurats.

Halley's Bible Handbook. Grand Rapids, MI: Zondervan, 2000, p. 100-102. The Tower of Babel may have looked like a Babylonian stepped pyramid.

Chapter 12. Abraham's Journeys
Good News Bible, Today's English Version. New York: American Bible Society, 1992. Genesis 12. Abram's Journeys.

Sanders, Nancy I. *Old Testament Days An Activity Guide.* Chicago: Chicago Review Press, 1999, p. 9-10. Background on Ur.

Boadt, Lawrence. *Reading the Old Testament.* New York: Paulist Press, 1984, p. 134-135. Travel and nomadic life.

Halley's Bible Handbook. Grand Rapids, MI: Zondervan, 2000, p. 110. Geography of Shechem.

Isbouts, Jean-Pierre. *The Biblical World: An Illustrated Atlas,* Washington, DC: National Geographic Society, 2007, p. 47-52. Background, travel time, Elamite arrival in Mesopotamia.

Reed Newland, Mary. *Written on Our Hearts,* Winona, MN: St. Mary's Press, 2002, p. 27. Dates for Abraham.

Joan Comay, *Who's Who in the Bible.* New York: Random House, 1971, p. 16, 28. Dates for Abraham.

https://www.metmuseum.org/toah/ht/03/wai.html Elamite invasion of Mesopotamia

Kagan, Neil, *A Concise History of the World,* Washington, DC: National Geographic Society, 2006, p. 47. Background.

Keller-Scholz, Rick & Pomanowski, Jeannie. *Break Through! The Bible for Young Catholics Teacher's Activity Manual.* Winona, MN: St. Mary's Press, 2006, p. 27-28. Thoughts about moving.

Chapter 13. Abraham's Sons

Good News Bible, Today's English Version. New York: American Bible Society, 1992. Genesis 15-21. Abraham's sons.

Genesis to Revelation. Nashville: Abington Press, 1997, p. 30 Slave inheritance.

Reed Newland, Mary. *A Popular Guide through the Old Testament.* Winona, MN: St. Mary's Press, 1999, p. 32 concubines.

Isbouts, Jean-Pierre. *The Biblical World, An Illustrated Atlas.* Washington, DC: National Geographic Society, 2007, p. 52. God—El and Yahweh, p. 63. Code of Hammurabi and marriage customs, p. 64. Polygamy, p. 72. Forefather of three faiths, p. 76: Shift from polytheism.

Chapter 14. Abraham Told to Sacrifice Isaac

Good News Bible, Today's English Version. New York: American Bible Society, 1992. Genesis 22. Abraham told to sacrifice Isaac.

Isbouts, Jean-Pierre. *The Biblical World: An illustrated Atlas.* Washington, DC: National Geographic Society, 2007 p. 73. Sacrifice of Isaac. Also, human sacrifice. p. 76: shift from polytheism.

Haney Schafer, Mary. *The Bible & Its Influence.* New York: BLP Publishing, 2006, p. 52. Sacrificing Isaac.

Buehrens, John. *Understanding the Bible.* Boston: Beacon Press, 203, p. 57-58. Human sacrifice in the ancient world. Muslim tradition: Ishmael was to be sacrificed.

Williams, Derek. *The Biblical Times.* Grand Rapids, MI: Baker Books, 1997. p. 41, Human sacrifice.

Reed Newland, Mary. *A Popular Guide through the Old Testament.* Winona, MN: St. Marty's Press, 1999,. p. 37. Abraham's unbelievable age at death.

Student Activity Workbook for Break Through. Winona, MN: St. Marty's Press, 2006. p. 26. A loving God did not approve of child sacrifices which was required by some polytheistic religions.

Chapter 15. Isaac

Good News Bible, Today's English Version. New York: American Bible Society, 1992. Genesis 24. Isaac.

Biblical Times. Williams, Derek. Grand Rapids, MI: Baker Books, 1997, p. 42. 400-mile journey.

Isbouts, Jean-Pierre. *The Biblical World: An illustrated Atlas.* Washington, DC: National Geographic Society, 2007, p. 88. Were there camels in Israel in Abraham's time?

Reed Newland, Mary. *A Popular Guide Through the OT.* Winona, MN: St. Mary's Press, 1999, p. 36. In Rebecca Isaac finds comfort after the death of his mother, p. 37. Abraham's age at death.

Chapter 16. Jacob and Esau

Good News Bible, Today's English Version. New York: American Bible Society, 1992, Genesis 25-28. Jacob and Esau.

Halley's Bible Handbook. Grand Rapids, MI: Zondervan, 2000, p. 119- 120. Birthrights (double portion) and blessings.

Geoghegan, Jeffery & Homan, Michael. *The Bible for Dummies*. Hoboken, NJ: John Wiley & Sons, 2003, p. 90. Blessings – a prediction of the future.

The Catholic Youth Bible. Winona, WI: Saint Mary's Press, 2000, p. 35. Birthrights & blessings: the oldest son.

Chapter 17. Jacob

Good News Bible, Today's English Version. New York: American Bible Society, 1992, Genesis 25-28. Jacob.

Halley's Bible Handbook. Grand Rapids, MI: Zondervan, 2000, p. 122. Jacob's return to his homeland after 20 years absence.

Williams, Derek. *The Bible Times*. Grand Rapids, MI: Baker Books, 1997, p. 46. Jacob's selective breeding of the herd.

Isbouts, Jean-Pierre. *The Biblical World: An Illustrated Atlas*. Washington, DC: National Geographic Society, 2007, p. 82. Stairway to heaven- ziggurats. p. 83. Average price for a bride in ancient Mesopotamia.

The Catholic Youth Bible. Winona, MN: Saint Mary's Press, 2000, p. 34. Jacob's human character – both good & bad…

Nichols, John. *A Wind Swept over Waters: Reflections on 60 Favorite Bible Passages*. Boston: Skinner House Books, 2007, p. 11. Decisions come from insights, conversions, or just courage.…

Chapter 18. Joseph & His Brothers

Good News Bible, Today's English Version. New York: American Bible Society, 1992, Genesis 37. Joseph and his brothers.

The Catholic Youth Bible. Winona, MN: Saint Mary's Press, 2000, p. 45. Broadway shows.

https://en.wikipedia.org/wiki/Joseph_and_the_Amazing_Technicolor_Dreamcoat. Number of productions.

Isbouts, Jean-Pierre. *The Biblical World, An Illustrated Atlas.* Washington, DC: National Geographic Society, 2007, p. 87, 88, 96. Trading spices, incorrect statement about the use of camels. Slavery, shekels.

Williams, Derek. *The Biblical Times.* Grand Rapids, MI: Baker Books, 1997, p. 48: Traders carried spices and cosmetic preparations.

Break Through! The Bible for Young Catholics, Winona, MN: St. Mary's Press, 2006, p. 53. Favoritism among siblings.

Gibbs Binkley, Cheryl & McKeel, Jane M. *Living the Promise.* Arlington, VA, Self-published by the Unitarian Church of Arlington, p. 48. The story of Joseph and its meaning.

The Bible and Its Influence, Teacher's Edition. Front Royal, VA: BLP Publishing, 2006, p. 57. Langages and customs.

Chapter 19. Joseph & the Wife of the Palace Guard

Good News Bible, Today's English Version. New York: American Bible Society, 1992, Genesis 39. Joseph and the wife of the captain of the palace guard.

Break Through! The Bible for Young Catholics. Winona, MN: Saint Mary's Press, 2006, p. 57. Joseph: accused of rape & imprisoned.

Gibbs Binkley, Cheryl & McKeel, Jane M., *Living the Promise.* Self-published with the Unitarian Church of Arlington, VA, p. 48 Overview.

Isbouts, Jean-Pierre. *The Biblical World, An Illustrated Atlas.* Washington, DC: National Geographic Society, 2007, p. 92. Background on Potiphar's wife.

Chapter 20. Joseph Interprets Dreams

Good News Bible, Today's English Version. New York: American Bible Society, 1992. Genesis 40-41. Joseph interprets dreams.

The Catholic Youth Bible. Winona, WI: Saint Mary's Press, 2000, p. 49. Dreams conveyed messages from their gods and needed interpretation.

http://www.crystalinks.com/egyptdreamscrying.html. Dreams bring messages from the gods.

http://www.ancient-origins.net/myths-legends/egyptian-dream-book-001621 Dreams place in Egyptian culture.

http://dreamhawk.com/dream-encyclopedia/egyptian-dream-beliefs. Dreams provide warnings and advice from the gods.

Isbouts, Jean-Pierre. *The Biblical World, An Illustrated Atlas*. Washington, DC: National Geographic Society, 2007, p. 95. Diet & dreams, p. 97 & 100. Famine and the pharaoh's responsibility.

Gibbs Binkley, Cheryl & McKeel, Jane M., *Living the Promise*. Self-published with the Unitarian Church of Arlington, VA, p. 56. Dreams – meaning today & then.

Williams, Derek. *The Biblical Times*, Grand Rapids, MI: Baker Books, 1997, p. 49. Rainfall & Nile River flooding cycles.

Chapter 21. Joseph's Brothers Go to Egypt & Return with Benjamin

Good News Bible, Today's English Version. New York: American Bible Society, 1992. Genesis 40-41. Joseph's brothers go to Egypt and return with Benjamin.

Isbouts, Jean-Pierre. *The Biblical World, An Illustrated Atlas*. Washington, DC: National Geographic Society, 2007, p. 94 Few Egyptians learned the foreign languages of their slaves. Instead the slaves had to learn the language and traditions of the Egyptians. p. 101 Coastal Highway travel time.

Gibbs Binkley, Cheryl & McKeel, Jane M., *Living the Promise*. Self-published with the Unitarian Church of Arlington, VA, p. 56. Decision 3: "When his brothers arrive, Joseph…

Genesis to Revelation, Teacher Book, Volume. Nashville: Abingdon Press, 1997, p. 61. Foreigners traveling to Egypt to buy grain.

Chapter 22. Missing Cup & Joseph Identifies Himself

Good News Bible, Today's English Version. New York: American Bible Society, 1992. Genesis 44-45. The missing cup and Joseph identifies himself.

Gibbs Binkley, Cheryl & McKeel, Jane M., *Living the Promise*. Self-published with the Unitarian Church of Arlington, VA, p. 56-57. How might the brothers have felt when Joseph identified himself?

Chapter 23. Jacob's Family Moves to Egypt & Famine Strikes Harder
Good News Bible, Today's English Version. New York: American Bible Society, 1992. Genesis 46-47. Jacob's family moves to Egypt, and famine strikes harder.

Isbouts, Jean-Pierre. *The Biblical World, An Illustrated Atlas*. Washington, DC: National Geographic Society, 2007, p. 103. Goshen was a well-irrigated pasture land.

Chapter 24. Jacob's Blessing & Death
Good News Bible, Today's English Version. New York: American Bible Society, 1992. Genesis 48-50. Jacob's last request, blessing, and death.

Feiler, Bruce. *Walking the Bible*. New York: William Marrow, 2001, p. 163. No evidence of Joseph in Egypt.

Genesis to Revelation, Vol. 1, Teacher Book. Nashville: Abington Press, 1997, p. 57. Lack of evidence of Joseph in Egypt.

Isbouts, Jean-Pierre. *The Biblical World, An Illustrated Atlas*. Washington, DC: National Geographic Society, 2007, p. 103-105. Israelites in Egypt and embalming.

Burstein, Stanley M. & Shek, Richard. *Ancient Civilizations through the Renaissance*. Orlando, FL: Houghton Mifflin Harcourt, 2012, p. 92-93. Embalming and burial customs.

Williams, Derek. *The Biblical Times*, Grand Rapids, MI: Baker Books, 1997, p. 51. Days of mourning.

Reed Newland, Mary. *Teaching Manual for Written on Our Hearts: The Old Testament Story of God's Love*, Winona, MN: Saint Mary's Press, 2002, p. 61: How do Joseph and his brothers grow in this story?

Chapter 25. Moses' Early Life
Good News Bible, Today's English Version. New York: American Bible Society, 1992. Exodus 1-4. Moses' early life.

Isbouts, Jean-Pierre. *The Biblical World, An Illustrated Atlas*. Washington, DC: National Geographic Society, 2007, p. 119. Moses' name; p. 108-115. Hyksos occupation.

Geoghegan, Jeffery & Homan, Michael,. *The Bible for Dummies*. Hoboken, NJ: John A. Wiley & Sons, 2003, p. 110-111 Moses' name, nursing practices, Midianites.

Feiler, Bruce. *Walking the Bible*. New York: HarperCollins, 2014, p. 168-169. Stories similar to Moses.

Armento, Beverly J. et al. *A Message of Ancient Days*. Boston: Houghton Mifflin, 2003, p. 396. Stories similar to Moses.

Haney Schafer, Marjorie. *The Bible and Its Influence*, Teacher's Edition. New York: BLP Publishing, 2006, p. 66. God's name.

Reed Newland, Mary. *Written on Our Hearts*. Winona, MN: Saint Mary's Press, 2002, p. 56. God's name.
Reed Newland, Mary. *A Popular Guide through the Old Testament*. Winona, MN: St. Mary's Press, 1999, p. 49, 50. God's name.

Gibbs Binkley, Cheryl & McKeel, Jane M., *Living the Promise*. Self-published with the Unitarian Church of Arlington, VA, p. 60, 62. God's name.

Chapter 26. Ten Plagues

Good News Bible, Today's English Version. New York: American Bible Society, 1992, Exodus 4-12. The ten plagues.

Reed Newland, Mary. *Written on Our Hearts*. Winona, MN: Saint Mary's Press, 2002, p. 57. The king accuses Moses of luring the Israelites from work.

Boadt, Lawrence. *Reading the Old Testament*. New York: Paulist Press, 1984, p. 167-168. Natural explanation for the nine plagues.

Feiler, Bruce. *Walking the Bible*. New York: HarperCollins, 2014, p. 182. Natural explanation for the nine plagues.

Isbouts, Jean-Pierre. *The Biblical World, An Illustrated Atlas*. Washington, DC: National Geographic Society, 2007, p. 125. Natural explanation for the nine plagues.

Halley's Bible Handbook. Grand Rapids, MI: Zondervan, 2000, p. 140. Symbol of power over the Egyptian gods.

Chapter 27. The Ten Commandments

Good News Bible, Today's English Version, New York: American Bible Society, 1992. Exodus 13-20, 24. The Ten Commandments.

Isbouts, Jean-Pierre. *The Biblical World, An Illustrated Atlas.* Washington, DC: National Geographic Society, 2007, p. 131. Coastal Hwy route; p. 134-135: Slave diet/desert diet. p. 136: Manna, El—symbol of virility & strength; p. 136: Mt Sinai, 7500 feet, gray and pink granite.

Sanders, Nancy I. *Old Testament Days, An Activity Guide.* Chicago: Chicago Review Press, 1999, p. 69. The Tabernacle.

Boadt, Lawrence. *Reading the Old Testament.* New York: Paulist Press, 1984, p.169 Reed Sea; p. 186: ancient codes similar to the Ten Commandments.

Feiler, Bruce. *Walking the Bible.* New York: HarperCollins, 2001, p. 174. No evidence of exodus. p. 206-207. Population est. 600,000 men, p. 220. Manna.

Gibbs Binkley, Cheryl & McKeel, Jane M., *Living the Promise.* Self-published with the Unitarian Church of Arlington, VA, p. 61, Mt Sinai hidden in clouds.

Halley's Bible Handbook. Grand Rapids, MI: Zondervan, 2000, p. 133. Coastal Highway fortifications, p. 137. Population estimate of 600,000 men. p. 141. Impact of Israelite slaves,.p. 145. Desert of Sin probably named for the Babylonian moon god, Sin.

Reed Newland, Mary. *Teaching Manual for Written on Our Hearts: The Old Testament Story of God's Love.* Winona, MN: Saint Mary's Press, 2002, p. 83. Symbol of blood.

Geoghegan, Jeffery & Homan, Michael. *The Bible for Dummies.* Hoboken, NJ: John A. Wiley & Sons, 2003, p. 115. Red Sea crossing. p. 120. Bull-calf was one-year bull.

Armento, Beverly J. et al. *A Message of Ancient Days.* Boston: Houghton Mifflin, 2003, p. 157-158, 172-173. Priests-kings, codes of law.

Chapter 28. Joshua

Good News Bible, Today's English Version. New York: American Bible Society, 1992. Joshua 1-6, 24. Joshua.

Isbouts, Jean-Pierre. *The Biblical World, An Illustrated Atlas*. Washington, DC: National Geographic Society, 2007, p. 143-146, 157. History, trumpets, housing.

Genesis to Revelation, Teacher Book. Nashville: Abington Press, 1997, p. 191. Explains why they are in exile.

Reed Newland, Mary. *A Popular Guide through the Old Testament*. Winona, MN: St. Mary's Press, 1999, p. 81. Need to return to God.

Gibbs Binkley, Cheryl & McKeel, Jane M., *Living the Promise*. Self-published with the Unitarian Church of Arlington, VA, p. 83. Example of Joshua's standards.

Chapter 29. Judges

Good News Bible, Today's English Version. New York: American Bible Society, 1992. Judges 4, 6, 16. Judges: Deborah, Gideon, and Samson.

Boadt, Lawrence. *Reading the Old Testament, An Introduction.* New York: Paulist Press, 1984, p. 199 co-existence; p. 214, Canaanite prosperity; p. 216-218, Canaanite gods; p. 223-224; Comparison of cultures.

A Popular Guide Through the Old Testament, p. 79-81, description of the Book of Judges; p. 93-95. Samson.

Comay, Joan. *Who's Who in the Bible.* New York: Wings Books, 1971, p. 62. Baal.

Halley's Bible Handbook. Grand Rapids, MI: Zondervan, 2000, p. 187-209. History of the Judges era; p. 202. The number forty.

Isbouts, Jean-Pierre. *The Biblical World, An Illustrated Atlas.* Washington, DC: National Geographic Society, 2007, p. 145 weapons.

Gibbs Binkley, Cheryl & McKeel, Jane M., *Living the Promise.* Self-Published with the Unitarian Church of Arlington, VA, p. 80. Farmer skit, p. 85 weapons.

Break Through! The Bible for Young Catholics. Winona, MN: Saint Mary's Press, 2006, p. 283. Why the Book of Judges was written.

Nichols, John. *A Wind Swept over the Waters,* Boston: Skinner House Books, 2007, p. 16-17. Idol worship today.

Chapter 30. Ruth

Good News Bible, Today's English Version. New York: American Bible Society, 1992. Ruth 1-4. Ruth.

Reed Newland, Mary. *A Popular Guide through the Old Testament.* Winona, MN: St. Mary's Press, 1999, p. 95-96, storytelling customs; p. 99, marriage customs.

Break Through! The Bible for Young Catholics. Winona, MN: Saint Mary's Press, 2006, p. 319. We do not know who wrote Ruth. Story of love and dedication.

Chapter 31. Samuel

Good News Bible, Today's English Version. New York: American Bible Society, 1992, p. 314. Introduction to Samuel. Samuel: 1 Samuel 1-2, 8-10.

Isbouts, Jean-Pierre. *The Biblical World, An Illustrated Atlas.* Washington, DC: National Geographic Society, 2007, p. 170-171. Excavations of pig bones – not in Israel but in Philistine and Transjordan.

Boadt, Lawrence. *Reading the Old Testament.* New York: Paulist Press, 1984, p. 246-250. Housing and towns. Daily life, sickness, afterlife.

Genesis to Revelation, Vol. 1, Teacher Book. Nashville: Abingdon Press, 1997, p. 257. Unknown author of 1 & 2 Samuel. Practice of sacrifices, p. 263. Farming practices and gods, Baal & Ashtoreth, p. 268. Kingships were common & thought to be divine, p. 322. Samuel & Kings originally one book in scrolls .Greek Septuagint used current names.

Break Through! The Bible for Young Catholics. Winona, MN: Saint Mary's Press, 2006, p. 340. Anointing with olive oil.

Geoghegan, Jeffery & Homan, Michael. *The Bible for Dummies.* Hoboken, NJ: John A. Wiley & Sons, 2003, p. 155. Pattern of women not able to get pregnant.

Kagan, Neil, *A Concise History of the World,* Washington, DC: National Geographic Society, 2006, p. 51. Saul anointed due to fear of Philistines.

Reed Newland, Mary. *A Popular Guide through the Old Testament.* Winona, MN: St. Mary's Press, 1999, p. 103. Overview of attacking Philistines. p. 108. Anointment of Saul, a familiar pattern: lowest, least likely.

Chapter 32. Samuel
Good News Bible, Today's English Version. New York: American Bible Society, 1992. 1 Samuel 11-16, Saul.

Comay, Joan. *Who's Who in the Bible.* New York: Wings Books, 1971, p. 326-330. Saul's home in Gibeah and his accomplishments.

Reed Newland, Mary. *A Popular Guide through the Old Testament.* Winona, MN: St. Mary's Press, 1999, p. 108. Only a priest could offer a sacrifice. Saul disobeys God twice.

Genesis to Revelation, Vol. 1, Teacher Book. Nashville: Abington Press, 1997, p. 262. Philistine settlements & war weapons & tactics, p. 287. Saul's accomplishments.

Chapter 33. Young David
Good News Bible, Today's English Version. New York: American Bible Society, 1992. 1 Samuel 17-31. Young David.

Geoghegan, Jeffery & Homan, Michael. *The Bible for Dummies.* Hoboken, NJ: John A. Wiley & Sons, 2003, p. 162. Sling and slingers.

Williams, Derek. *The Biblical Times.* Grand Rapids, MI: Baker Books, 1997, p. 97. Sling;.

Genesis to Revelation, Vol. 1, Teacher Book. Nashville: Abington Press, 1997, p. 262. Philistine settlements, war weapons & tactics. Location of the Ark of the Covenant.

Reed Newland, Mary. *A Popular Guide through the Old Testament.* Winona, MN: St. Mary's Press, 1999, p. 111. The story of the David-Jonathan friendship.

Break Through! The Bible for Young Catholics. Winona, MN: Saint Mary's Press, 2006, p. 354. David and Jonathan are very close friends.
Gibbs Binkley, Cheryl & McKeel, Jane M., *Living the Promise.* Self-published with the Unitarian Church of Arlington, VA, p. 98. Friendship: Have you ever had to depend on a friend for a major matter?

Chapter 34. David's Reign
Good News Bible, Today's English Version. New York: American Bible Society, 1992. 2 Samuel 2-7, 11-12 Samuel David's reign.

Genesis to Revelation, Vol. 1, Teacher Book. Nashville: Abington Press, 1997, p. 257. Religious sites, p. 263. Symbol of the Covenant Box, p. 293. Significance of Hebron, p. 297 & 316. Israel under David, p. 299. Anti-temple tradition in the *Old Testament,* p. 303. Israel's wealth.

Break Through! The Bible for Young Catholics. Winona, MN: Saint Mary's Press, 2006, p. 379. Jerusalem as a holy city for three religions.

Reed Newland, Mary. *A Popular Guide through the Old Testament.* Winona, MN: St. Mary's Press, 1999, p. 114. David's rule of first Judah and then all Israel, p. 115. Jerusalem as a holy city for three religions. Advantages of Jerusalem as a capital.

Isbouts, Jean-Pierre. *The Biblical World, An Illustrated Atlas.* Washington, DC: National Geographic Society, 2007, p. 187. David's authorship of Psalms.

Comay, Joan. *Who's Who in the Bible.* New York: Wings Books, 1971, p. 97. David's authorship of Psalms.

Chapter 35. David's Sons
Good News Bible, Today's English Version. New York: American Bible Society, 1992. 2 Samuel 13-19. David's out of control sons.

Chapter 36. Solomon
Good News Bible, Today's English Version. New York: American Bible Society, 1992, 1 Kings 1-11. Solomon.

Boadt, Lawrence, *Reading the Old Testament.* New York: Paulist Press, 1984, p. 237. Solomon's accomplishments, p. 245. Israel's transition.

Reed Newland, Mary. *A Popular Guide through the Old Testament.* Winona, MN: St. Mary's Press, 1999, p. 122-126. Trade routes, nation organized by 12 districts not by tribe, writings.

Hartley, Linda. *Israel Ancient Civilization Series.* Grand Rapids, MI: McGraw Hill Children's Publishing, 1997, p. 42. Temple construction facts.

Sanders, Nancy I. *Old Testament Days, An Activity Guide.* Chicago: Chicago Review Press, 1999, p. 128. Temple courtyard and furnishings.

Isbouts, Jean-Pierre. *The Biblical World, An Illustrated Atlas.* Washington, DC: National Geographic Society, 2007, p. 195. The Temple was later destroyed.

(http://www.pbs.org/mythsandheroes/myths_four_sheba.html). Queen of Sheba: travel, trade, gifts, visit.

Genesis to Revelation, Vol. 1, Teacher Book. Nashville: Abington Press, 1997, p. 322. Probably more than one writer; p. 326. Foreign marriages—political & military purposes.

Comay, Joan. *Who's Who in the Bible.* New York: Wings Books, 1971, p. 348-358. Background info on Solomon.

Chapter 37. Esther

Good News Bible, Today's English Version. New York: American Bible Society, 1992. Esther 1-9. Esther, King Xerxes, Mordecai, and Haman.

Haney Schafer, Marjorie. *The Bible and Its Influence*, Teacher's Edition. New York: BLP Publishing, 2006, p. 172. Background on the Book of Esther.

Genesis to Revelation, Vol. 1, Teacher Book. Nashville: Abington Press, 1997, p. 429. Origin of Purim. Concern for inclusion in holy scriptures. Themes.

Reed Newland, Mary. *Written on Our Hearts.* Winona, MN: Saint Mary's Press, 2002, p. 261. Esther is fictional. Xerxes real.

Armento, Beverly J. et al, *A Message of Ancient Days*, Boston: Houghton Mifflin, 2003, p. 355-356. King Xerxes background.

Buehrens, John A., *Understanding the Bible.* Beacon Press: Boston, 2003, p. 125. Reluctance to include in holy scriptures. Dates of celebration.

About the Author

Kenneth E. Walsh taught the Old Testament for 14 years at St. Ignatius Loyola Academy, Baltimore, MD, a tuition-free, Jesuit, inner-city middle school for boys from low-income families. Typically, fewer than five percent of the students were Catholic; and, while most claimed to be Christian, fewer than half attended church. Some attended a mosque. Some practiced no religion.

While he initially taught the Old Testament stories from a historical perspective so as not to offend anyone, he gradually added universal lessons that all of the students could identify with regardless of their religious background. He taught for all and sought to offend no one. Upon his retirement he decided to write a *Bible* stories book for all, religious and non-religious, based on his classroom experience and additional research.

Prior to his teaching career, he worked 34 years in the Social Security Administration starting as a claims representative in local offices and advancing to several senior management positions in the areas of facilities, disability claims, earnings records, and online electronic services.

He graduated from St. Pius X Preparatory Seminary, Uniondale, NY; the University of Pittsburgh with a B.A. degree in Political Science and Economics; and, later in life with M.Ed. in Curriculum & Instruction from Loyola College of Maryland. In his church he taught Sunday school from second grade through high school. He has served as a past president of the Owen Brown Interfaith Center, Columbia, MD.